DO
LEMONS
HAVE
FEATHERS?

of related interest

When Herscue Met Jomphrey and Other
Tales from an Aspie Marriage
Herscue Bergenstreiml
ISBN 978 1 84905 696 0
eISBN 978 1 78450 211 9

The Obsessive Joy of Autism
Julia Bascom
Illustrated by Elou Carroll
ISBN 978 1 84905 726 4
eISBN 978 1 78450 150 1

Nerdy, Shy, and Socially Inappropriate
A User Guide to an Asperger Life
Cynthia Kim
ISBN 978 1 84905 757 8
eISBN 978 0 85700 949 4

DAVID J. BURNS
FOREWORD BY ANDREW SERCOMBE

DO
LEMONS
HAVE
FEATHERS?

MORE TO AUTISM THAN
MEETS THE EYE

Jessica Kingsley *Publishers*
London and Philadelphia

First published in 2016
by Jessica Kingsley Publishers
73 Collier Street
London N1 9BE, UK
and
400 Market Street, Suite 400
Philadelphia, PA 19106, USA

www.jkp.com

Library of Congress Cataloging in Publication Data
Names: Burns, David J., author.
Title: Do lemons have feathers? : more to autism than meets the eye / David
 J. Burns ; foreword by Andrew Sercombe
Description: London ; Philadelphia : Jessica Kingsley Publishers, 2016.
Identifiers: LCCN 2015038813 | ISBN 9781785920134 (alk. paper)
Subjects: LCSH: Burns, David J.,--Mental health. | Autistic
 people--Biography. | Autism--Social aspects.
Classification: LCC RC553.A88 B872 2016 | DDC 616.85/882--
dc23 LC record available at http://lccn.loc.gov/2015038813

British Library Cataloguing in Publication Data
A CIP catalogue record for this book is available from the British Library

ISBN 978 1 78592 013 4
eISBN 978 1 78450 254 6

Printed and bound in Great Britain

To Hannah.
I'm so proud of you.

Contents

Foreword

I read this book in one sitting. I couldn't help myself. It is compelling reading. It takes you on a roller-coaster ride of discovery. It is unputdownable. Brilliant. Deep. Light. Easy reading. Challenging. Loving. Charged with priceless insight. Wise. Inspiring. And more.

I've known David for 30 years. He is highly intelligent, hilarious – lethally so when you get to know him! – and a really loyal and kind friend, but, to be honest, I didn't realise he was such a gifted writer. Knowing him as I do, I suspect he didn't realise either but just decided to put his life on the line so that others who experience more or less autism – either themselves or through someone they know, love, teach or work with – will understand. Or understand better. Typical.

I can vouch for David J. Burns' integrity. I've watched his journey, the humility, love and courage that exudes from his life, and have been challenged by the determination and generosity of a life devoted to helping others. What he writes is naked truth. The challenges he has faced are real. The situations of which he writes are authentic – as described.

David is now in increasingly high demand as a consultant, speaker and advocate for those in the 'autistic world' as people in education, work and family relationship contexts are finding out that what this man has to say is changing minds and hearts.

As you read this book, let his words change your mind and heart too. You'll soon notice that the book is written by someone who is high-functioning autistic. I challenge you not to laugh out loud as you make your way through to the particularly insightful final chapters. And when you get to the end, like me, you'll feel that sense of being honoured with a glimpse into the life – and privacy – of a brave man.

Andrew Sercombe
www.powerchange.com

Acknowledgements

My thanks must go to the many parents I have met who have shared their stories. I know it has not been easy for you, and many of you face an uphill struggle for support with your child's autism. I'm grateful for all you've shared – your children are amazing people.

I'd like to thank Moyra. She has encouraged me to write this book and produce something for everyone. It would have been so easy to never start writing, but after an initial draft chapter she said, 'I want more!'

To the Tuesday Billingshurst autism support group I say, 'Thank you for welcoming me and making me realise I can bring hope.' Our times together have helped me to see what I needed to include in this edition and your feedback on the draft chapters has been enormously helpful.

I'm also grateful to Uta Frith for her kind words of endorsement on the front cover. Uta Frith is Emeritus Professor of Cognitive Development at UCL. Among other books and articles on autism spectrum conditions, she has written *Autism: A Very Short Introduction*. Recently, she presented the BBC Horizon documentary *Living with Autism*.

Lastly, I'd like to tell you more about my friend, Andrew Sercombe. I mention at times what 'my friend' might say and Andrew has been perhaps the most supportive and encouraging friend I've known in the last 30 years.

I've repeated some of the things he's taught me that were memorable and which I thought people might find helpful.

Andrew runs a professional development company unlike any other. It's called Powerchange and he continues to bless and change lives pretty much every day. You can find out more about Andrew and his work by visiting his website at www.powerchange.com.

I've included some summary Help Sheets at the end of the book which many have said have been really useful to families and schools in understanding autism. There is also a request asking you to help others using your own social media contacts to make the book known to them. If you are able to respond, then I want to thank you in advance.

David

1

Do Lemons Have Feathers?

'I was able to do certain things *because* of autism and not *in spite of* autism.'

DAVID J. BURNS

I love stories! Don't you? I recently heard the story about a guest at a party who'd had too much to drink.

He approached the host and asked the following question:

'Do lemons have feathers?'

'I beg your pardon?' the host replied.

'Do lemons have feathers?'

'Of course they don't!' the host exclaimed.

'Oh dear. Then I think I've just squeezed your pet canary into my drink.'

I found it really funny because I'm a natural when it comes to the social faux pas. I'm socially awkward and I guess at times people would say I'm a bit like a 'lemon'.

As I thought about the story and the question posed, I began to see something else. The question 'Do lemons have feathers?' challenged me to think about my life and whether or not there was more to someone with autism than meets the eye.

Shoppers recognise a lemon by its colour and shape, rarely by its smell or what it looks like on the inside. Indeed, I've never seen someone in a supermarket pick up a lemon and check it's a lemon by putting it to their nose or slicing it in half. It is what it is, they conclude, and put it in their basket without any further thought.

We all know they are used in food and drink, but I wonder if you know the following facts about lemons? A lemon really is a fabulous fruit!

- They are thought to have originated in northeast India – not Italy, France or Florida.

- A study of the genetic origin of the lemon shows it to be a hybrid of a bitter orange and a citron.

- Originally, lemons were mainly used as an ornamental plant and for medicine.

- Lemons have a short-term preservative effect.

- The juice can be used for removing grease and can clean stains from clothes.

- The low pH of the juice makes it antibacterial and is helpful to fight illness.

- The oil from the peel is used in wood cleaner and polish, where its solvent properties dissolve old wax, fingerprints and dirt.

- Lemons contain the following nutrients and minerals:

  - thiamine (B1)

  - riboflavin (B2)

  - niacin (B3)

  - pantothenic acid (B5)

  - vitamin B6

  - folate (B9)

  - vitamin A

  - vitamin C

  - vitamin E

  - calcium

  - iron

  - magnesium

  - manganese

  - phosphorus

- potassium

- zinc.

🌿 Lemon balm has a calming effect and it is believed that breathing in lemon oil can improve concentration and alertness.

🌿 A lemon's coagulant properties can help to stop bleeding.

🌿 Lemon juice can be used as invisible ink, which can then be revealed by heat.

When it comes to Asperger's or high-functioning autism, it's easy to just see the condition and all the negative associations we read about in the press. However, if we're to change perceptions, reduce prejudice and help those with autism, we have to discover the benefits. Folks, it's time to stop looking at the obvious and start looking for the significant. Along with the difficulties autism brings, there are definite benefits.

I was diagnosed some years ago as an adult on the autistic spectrum. I always knew I was different and didn't quite fit in. Although I'd tried to overcome the social awkwardness I felt inside, believing it to be natural shyness, I never really managed it. I wanted to have friends and be accepted, but I just couldn't work out how to do this or know if people liked me. When the diagnosis arrived, I began to understand that what I struggled with had a reason. I focussed, to begin with, on accepting myself just as I was. I'm not a victim and I don't suffer from autism, but I do understand my limitations. I don't pretend to be what I'm not. I then began to recognise that my autism had its strengths. I was able to do certain things *because* of autism and not *in spite of* autism. I began to see autism as a gift to be used.

When someone says they have Asperger's syndrome, the usual response from people is either silence or sympathy. However, my response is to say, 'That's great! What are the advantages of having Asperger's?' What I've found is that, after the shock of the question, the person in front of me starts to change the way they think. That marks a new beginning for them.

Some of my children are on the spectrum and autism has been an integral part of family life. However, each child is an individual with a different personality, different challenges and different strengths. I've had to get to know each of them separately and adjust how I do things. I've enjoyed great times and I've been through some pretty rotten times raising the family. However, I believe I have an insight and experience that can help others.

On more than one occasion people have said to me that my life brings them hope, and when someone says something as important as that, I know I need to do something to reach out to others. That's why I've written this book. I want to help, comfort and bring hope to as many people as I can, especially you. I've included subjects people have asked me about and answered questions about behaviour people don't understand along with suggestions as to what to do. (Sometimes doing nothing is the best option.)

You're probably reading this book either because you're someone with an autism condition or because you're a parent or a teacher of a child with autism or maybe know someone who is gifted in this way. Fundamentally, I want to encourage you because we all face tough times. A diagnosis of autism is one thing, but living a fulfilling life is quite another. That applies to the person with the condition and their family. Can you just pause for a moment and pretend I'm right beside you? Great. Knowing you're facing some real challenges, right now I want to tell you something.

To the reader with autism I want to say, 'Your life matters.'

To the parent who's struggling with a child with autism I want to say, 'You're not alone.'

To the teacher facing a child with challenging behaviour I want to say, 'Your continued support and encouragement is life-changing.'

I've chosen these words because they represent perhaps the most prominent things I encounter when I talk to people with autism, parents or teachers. Many with Asperger's-type autism wonder what life will hold for them and if their life is worth living, because people treat them as if they should be able to behave in exactly the same way as everyone else. They've not yet discovered the beauty within and the difference they can make in the world. I believe their life matters.

Parents, on the other hand, feel alone. The diagnosis doesn't solve the issues and quite often marks the beginning of their struggles. They face the fallout of their child's actions and feel isolated from others. The one thing that's consistent is that they don't know what tomorrow will bring. A phone call from the school, a three-day exclusion or a fight in the park. Yet, just because their child's behaviour may seem awful, it doesn't make them a bad parent. It's not their fault.

Behaviour resulting from sensory overload is just that – behaviour. Many people face similar situations so I believe they are not alone.

Teachers struggle with how to manage a class with a child who cannot follow the school's behaviour policy. There are daily incidents and strategies they were told that just don't seem to work. I remember those teachers who encouraged me and showed great patience. They understood my difficulties, and although autism wasn't widely diagnosed when I was a child, some teachers were kind to me. They decided what was important and what was just plain stupid or immature. They worked out what I needed to be spoken to about and where I needed help. I particularly remember my maths teacher. His kindness, support and encouragement was life-changing.

The autism I have is at the high-functioning end of the spectrum. Previously it might have been called Asperger's syndrome, but now I believe the correct term is autism spectrum condition. I can only speak with confidence about this end of the spectrum, and severe autism isn't something for which I can devise tried-and-tested strategies from my experience as a person with autism or as a parent raising children on the spectrum. However, I think I can at least encourage you and share in such a way that will enable you to see that we all face tough times and we can do it together. People who care are such a blessing.

I don't have an answer as to why I have autism or why you face what you do. Life sometimes seems unfair, but I believe that some of the things we face help to build character and enable us to help others. I love watching films based on true stories, and if you've ever watched *Zulu*, you might recall how a regiment of British soldiers survived an encounter with a Zulu army that far outnumbered them. One of my favourite parts is the reply that comes when Private Thomas Cole asks Colour Sergeant Bourne, 'Why is it us? Why us?'

Bourne replies, 'Because we're here, lad. Nobody else. Just us.'

Sometimes there's no reason except that we're here. There's no one to blame and you've not done something wrong. It just is. Having said that, I'd like to think that we can bring the best out of ourselves and others, and I've shared some tips I think you'll find useful, although it's entirely up to you what you decide to do with them. I could have focussed purely on the disadvantages of autism, but I've deliberately taken a positive and uplifting approach because I think, like other parents I've met, you'd rather I brought you hope. If you have an autism condition, you'll notice I've set about to encourage you to take a few brave steps. Please don't give up, because, as I've found, a step at a time begins a fabulous journey to personal freedom.

One last thing. I've added a good dose of humour to what I've written because sometimes it's just what the doctor ordered. Laughter is a great release and is good for us. So please laugh out loud – my stories and mishaps are there for you to enjoy.

2

It's Not What I Planned

'Everybody
is a genius. But if
you judge a fish by its ability
to climb a tree, it will live its whole life
believing that it is stupid.'

*ATTRIBUTED TO
ALBERT EINSTEIN*

Autism doesn't run in my family – it practically gallops! Its characteristics can be found in distant relatives and those closer to home, and it was no surprise when I was diagnosed as an adult. A little late, perhaps, but it was incredibly liberating nonetheless.

'Welcome to the world of autism!' I was told. 'Be kind to yourself.' Good advice.

Now, I want to ask you a question. Ready? Here goes!

Whose fault is it that I have autism?

I ask this question because most parents I meet blame themselves for the condition their children have, whether it's autism or something else. They decide they are going to take a guilt trip that lasts many years and costs their emotions dearly. I don't know of any parent who doesn't do it, and when I recently spoke to a mother, I found she still blamed herself even though her son was in his 20s. Yet it doesn't have to be like that. I want to ask you another question. Ready? Here goes!

When are you going to choose to stop blaming yourself?

Is your son or daughter blaming you or complaining? Is your family pointing the finger in your direction? Have the doctors issued you with a letter squarely laying the blame at your feet? You do have a choice and I want to help you. You've suffered for too long.

In the film *Forrest Gump*, Tom Hanks plays a man with autism. It's a great film and at the end he has a son who does not have autism. A happy ending! I like the T-shirt slogan that says, 'Leave me alone. I'm enjoying my happily ever after.' But I know life's not like that. It's tough: things go wrong and people don't always live happily ever after. Some of my children follow in my footsteps or have other conditions that could put them at a disadvantage. If anyone had reason to blame themselves for their children having autism, it would be me. I could blame myself and they certainly have every right to blame me. Thing is, just as I've never blamed my family for the way I am, so my children have never blamed me for the way they are. Honest.

Let me tell you something. Ready? Here goes!

It's not your fault

Get it? Really, it's not your fault. Let that sink in for a moment. I've never entertained the thought of blaming anyone for my autism, and I bet your son or daughter has never considered blaming you. Most parents I say this to usually shed a few tears. That's okay. It's high time the guilt trip came to an end. Take a trip to the next town. Take a trip to another county. Take a trip abroad. But please don't take a guilt trip. This is the next stop and I'm waiting. Will you get off the bus and walk with me for a while? I want to share a few things with you.

If I was to tell you one thing I've learned that has helped me to see beyond a condition as a disability, it would be this: I've learned to take advantage of my disadvantage. This, I believe, is key. Without autism I doubt I could write this book, encourage others and bring a unique insight based on my experience. I have come to believe that, in my case, I have an advantage, and I've met others who feel the same about their condition. I know someone with dyslexia who has very good spatial awareness when it comes to working out what fits into spaces. They have told me they would not want to stop having dyslexia because they believe they have some positive compensating traits. I'm no expert but I'm glad they have a positive outlook on what makes them different. And, no, we're not mutants with superpowers as in the film *X-Men*!

In this world everyone is unique, everyone is different. I love that. In fact, to me, normal is that we're all different. That means I can fit in somewhere. It's easy to see the obvious but a little tricky to discover the significant. It's okay to be different, so please don't feel guilty that your child is not the same as everyone else.

That doesn't mean we pretend that everything is fine, that there won't be issues and that things will be easy. What sort of person pretends everything is wonderful when it isn't? On the contrary, being true, honest and real about what we face is important. Like every Boy Scout who wants to meet a Girl Scout, being prepared is a good idea! Life is tough and getting through with 'true grit' (real determination) takes more than someone like John Wayne. Yet I'm convinced we can choose not to become a victim but to help others even in our heartache. An outlook that involves supporting others who face similar situations not only encourages them but also raises our spirits.

I'm also aware that a long-term problem may require a long-term solution. Let me explain.

There are days when I wonder how on earth I'll make it through. I bet you've been there too, haven't you? It's been tough for us at home, or school has sent a letter about how our children have misbehaved, or we've been misunderstood by a friend, or work has left us feeling undervalued. The list can be endless.

I remember a story about a lady whose husband hardly ever bought her flowers. But one day he decided he'd show her how much he appreciated her. On his way home he bought the most beautiful bouquet of flowers he could afford. Meanwhile, unbeknown to him, his wife had had one of those nightmare days. She was not ready for his kindness, and when he turned up with flowers, she burst into tears. 'What's wrong?' he enquired.

'I've had the most awful day,' she replied. 'The dog has been sick on the new carpet, your mother says she is coming to stay at the weekend and the kids have been nothing but trouble. The vacuum cleaner broke down this morning and spread filth everywhere, the car won't start, and to top it all you come home drunk!'

Sometimes even when something great comes along, we miss the good intentions and assume the worst. That's why I try to remember that although there will be tough days, there will always be great days. I'm in this for the long haul. It's called 'perseverance', not 'magic'.

The man who invented the light bulb, Thomas Edison, once said, 'Just because something doesn't do what you planned it to do doesn't mean it's useless.' I like that. It means that although I or others might not do what society expects, it doesn't mean we're useless. Your child is not useless. How come? Because you're there. You make the difference for the long term. Remember, a long-term problem may require a long-term solution. You are part of that solution.

Can I share something else? It took me a long time to learn this and I want to provide you with a shortcut. This is a journey that needs to be shortened and it's the journey to discover something really important. 'What is it?' you ask. It's this: both you and your child matter. Read that again. You matter. Your child matters.

Someone once asked me why I choose to help and encourage people who perhaps have no voice or are ignored by society or could be classed as being on the losing team because the odds are stacked against them. My response was, and has always been, 'Because they matter.'

One last thing. People are an essential ingredient in life. Leave the door of your life open to receive help. Don't pretend everything is fine when it's not. Old people are quite good at telling others how they are and maybe we ought to learn something from them – 'Oh, my varicose veins are a nightmare! It's like fire in my tights.'

Anyway, I love the story about the hyena and the monkey. It goes like this.

A hyena is walking along and he meets his friend the monkey. 'Hello, Hyena,' the monkey says. 'How are you today?'

'Oh, I'm okay but a bit fed up,' the hyena replies.

'Why are you fed up?' asks the monkey.

'Well, every day when I go home, a lion jumps out from the bushes and pushes me around. He thinks it's funny, you see. I'm sick of it,' the hyena explains.

'Oh dear!' exclaims the monkey. 'Tell you what, I'll walk home with you today, and if the lion jumps out, I'll help you.'

The hyena smiles. 'Would you do that for me? Thank you. You're a real friend.'

Well, that evening, as the monkey and the hyena walk through the jungle, the lion jumps out and gives a huge roar. The monkey, as scared as anyone would be, runs straight up a tree and watches from the top branch.

As on previous occasions, the lion proceeds to grab hold of the hyena and throw him about, treating him very roughly. Then, after about half an hour, the lion gets bored and walks off.

When the coast is clear, the monkey comes down from the tree and sits next to the hyena.

Through one blackened eye the hyena surveys the monkey and says, 'Fat lot of good you were! I thought you were here to help me?'

And the monkey replies, 'Well, you were laughing so much I thought you were enjoying it!'

Outward appearances can hide the turmoil we feel. Find a friend you can confide in. And if there's no one around to help, please believe that I am writing this chapter for you because it's the best way I know to remind you that you're not alone.

Life isn't meant to be a DIY project.

Can I help you?

Let me summarise the things I've been talking about. Ready? Great!

- It's not your fault. Don't do the guilt trip thing, or at least cut it short.

- Normal is that we're all different. It's okay that your child doesn't conform.

- You and your child really do matter.

- Be real and honest about the problems you face.

- A long-term problem may require a long-term solution. You are part of that solution.

- Although there will be tough days, remember that there will be great days too.

- Let others help you and seek encouragement when you need it.

3

The Angst of School Days

'I've never let my school interfere with my education.'

ATTRIBUTED TO MARK TWAIN

'Don't be a fool all your life – have a day off!' These were the words that echoed down the corridors of one of the schools my parents said I was 'fortunate' enough to attend.

Many modern schools have mottos such as 'Excellence and Achievement' or 'Encourage and Inspire'. These, I think, aim to reassure parents and create a sense of wonder. However, back in my school days we had no such reassurances. Most mottos could have read 'Take a chance on us'. If my school had adopted a motto, it could have easily consisted of the words 'Knock some sense into the blighters.' Being teacher's pet meant being locked in a cage at the back of the class, and children were an unfortunate inconvenience to the efficient running of the school.

I have to admit that entering a secondary school as a 12-year-old was one of the most traumatic events of my life. More terrifying than a charging rhino on heat, those school days advanced too quickly towards me. It was the process of coping with the enormous change in my surroundings and learning new unspoken rules that caused me great anxiety. I never knew I had to walk on the left-hand side or stand when a teacher entered the room. However, expectations became apparent when I heard raised voices and cries of 'Sorry, sir.' And raised voices always made me afraid. Indeed, I can remember checking school bags four or five times in the middle of the night to ensure I had everything for the next day because I was anxious I would forget something and be shouted at. That's another interesting observation. It seemed that seeing was not believing. Somehow the connection between *seeing* something in my bag and then *knowing* it was there took several attempts. Checking things once was not enough. Fortunately, no one stopped me from doing this and my anxiety subsided after about the fifth time I looked in my bag. Had I been stopped, I would have become distressed. Parents and teachers might worry about some obsessive behaviours, but sometimes it's better to ignore them because they may disappear when the circumstances causing them change. Once I'd left school, I no longer checked my bag.

It's true I was naturally timid. Why, you could have had a reign of terror over me with a balloon on a stick. It appeared to everyone else I was either shy or lacked confidence. Both were true and both were compounded by my inability to understand the world around me and engage with it. Not fitting in came easily to me, and it seemed that whatever I became involved with would always go wrong. I think the cause was not solely due to being hemmed in by my own incompetence. It had more to do with not foreseeing consequences and not having the strength of character to resist the influence of others. Saying no was difficult and I was frequently left as the last man standing in the midst of trouble while everyone else scarpered.

However, I am pleased to report that I did at least fit into one social circle. I say 'fit' because I automatically became part of the social outcasts and lepers group. We met every lunchtime – just the two of us. We were the ones no one would allow to be their imaginary friend. Thing is, we didn't know why we were outcasts. Nobody explained the rules of friendship to us.

I later found out that, at this particular school, friendships were forged on the basis of whether or not you looked cool but slightly scruffy, had a previous record of popularity or crime and were extroverted. I had neither a criminal record nor cool looks. My mother ensured I was smart, and I was born introverted.

There were some kind souls who treated me with gentleness, although I think they were under orders to assist defenceless animals or something. I couldn't tell from one day to the next who liked me and who didn't – they all resembled characters from the card game Happy Families, but no one seemed happy to see me.

I dreaded team games. Why? It was the humiliation of being the last to be picked because I was just too clumsy and poorly coordinated for anything that required the use of my feet and a ball. I recall many times when I was passed a ball near the goal and missed because I either tripped or was just plain nervous. Defence was the best position, where I learned to avoid any form of action. This is kind of strange when I had a history of family football players – my great-great-grandfather played for Swansea and Liverpool. My tactic of running away from the ball earned me disgrace and relegation, and I spent most of my sports lessons running around the outside of the field.

I guess secondary school is quite memorable to most people, but I can remember further back than that. I can remember playgroup and my first school days. Even in those early days, friendships were hard to forge and I frequently annoyed staff by a constant need to visit the lavatory. I've since heard that many children with autism find controlling these essential functions a challenge, and my memories are of being disciplined for needing to go so often or having great anxiety before any school trip because I wanted to know if there was a lavatory nearby.

Apparently, I was quite vocal with teachers about home life, much to the inconvenience of my parents. My mother recalls a time when she was called in to speak about the state of her marriage, after I, the little sod, had blurted out that my father was sleeping on the sofa. The head teacher said that she was very sorry to hear that my mother was having marital difficulties and was there for support should my mother need it. I understand it all turned out fine in the end and my observations, though correct, did not portray the whole truth of the situation. Although the head teacher had arrived at quite an understandable conclusion, my mother explained further that my father was sleeping on the sofa because he had a cold and snored rather loudly.

This illustrates the need to dig a bit deeper when you hear a story from any child and especially if they have autism. You'll probably only hear part of the tale and draw the wrong conclusions. They may not be articulate enough to explain what's happened, especially if they are anxious. It is easy to misinterpret something they say or forget they are vulnerable because other children make statements that are untrue but more articulate. The child with autism quite often stands alone with no one to support or help them explain, and you may only hear what they think you want to be told. Faced with their poor explanation and the assertions of another group of children, it's natural to go with the majority. Please don't automatically do that. Make a conscious choice to think differently and ask more questions. There are people with autism in prison because they have said what others want to hear or have been poorly instructed by solicitors. Be aware that there is a real vulnerability because communication is difficult.

When I was younger, I would share observations and say things as I saw them without realising that my statements were leading others to make conclusions I neither saw nor intended. It was like throwing a china tea set in the air, walking away and leaving others to try to decide what to do next. I'm sure there was plenty of fallout from my comments but I never realised or foresaw it. Today it can be a real art form and quite comedic in its results. I just love to watch and see if anyone takes the stuff I say out of context and ends up with the wrong end of the stick. I can also twist the meaning of a conversation with very funny results. Back in my school days, I couldn't do that so easily.

At school there were so many rules. I must have broken most of them because I frequently found myself in the head teacher's office even though I didn't always understand why. Thankfully, some took pity on me, particularly in 1979, as it was the Year of the Child and nobody wanted to seem cruel! As we get older, it can be useful to unlearn rules we obeyed as children. The principles may still be relevant but the rules no longer apply. It is my belief that to enable the transition between childhood and adulthood for the teenager with Asperger's or high-functioning autism, parents, carers and teachers need to actively help them to let go of some of the rules, give them permission to explore options and allow them to learn to make their own decisions and mistakes. Letting go is difficult for both the teenager and the parent, but I think love means I will choose to help set my children free.

We all have memories of school dinners and I was (and still am) a fussy eater. It has to do with texture. I find textured soups and mashed potato difficult to stomach, and the latter was a school staple. What was worse was that most school dinner ladies were remnants from the War and believed you should be grateful for anything. I was only ever grateful when lunch was over. The dread of warm beans, lumpy mashed potato and sausages made any maths lesson seem like a welcome distraction. Wherever possible, I avoided shepherd's pie, cottage pie, mashed potato, mushy peas, rice pudding or semolina. I felt safer if I could recognise what it started out like when it hit my plate rather than try to guess. And boy, did it hit my plate at speed! Mrs Sage, the dinner lady, was the fastest meal server in the whole of Surrey. The only time I enjoyed school dinner was at Christmas time. The teachers would serve us. Although this was fun, I couldn't abide Christmas pudding. On one occasion (and the only occasion!) a teacher forced me to eat it. I told her I would be sick, but she insisted. So I forced the mush of white vanilla sauce and fruit sponge down my throat. Less than 30 seconds later, the table was cleared of screaming children as the pudding returned at quite some speed. Well, I was always taught to be true to my word.

I mentioned earlier that I was quite shy and lacked confidence. Some of this has to do with the difficulties I faced trying to understand instructions, getting things wrong and then being reprimanded by teachers. Not all teachers were harsh, but it only took one to scare me. If you're a teacher, I'd like you to note especially the following formula because it can help you when communicating to 'pre-people' (children). Believe it or not, the quality of the result is directly proportional to the quality of the instruction. Conversely, the quality of the result is inversely proportional to how vague the instruction is. Yes, I like mathematics and formulae!

So what do I mean? Well, imagine I'm just eight years old and you ask me to draw a circle on a piece of paper. I probably won't complete the task or will be the last one to finish. If I'm not afraid of you, I'll ask you if I am doing it right, several times to make sure, and this will annoy you. I don't lack ability or intelligence. So what's the problem when everyone else can complete the task but I cannot? The answer, I'm pleased to say, is really simple. The instruction needs more clarity. By keeping the instruction void of any detail, my mind is asking questions and trying to compute and interpret what the result should be. If you don't bring clarity, I'll keep asking every step of the way, and I'll probably keep asking the same question until my mind registers that I understand the response or until the connection is made between the task and what you've said. Sometimes it takes my mind longer to connect things together and I can't see what you want because the request is too vague or you don't slow down what you are saying. I know what a circle is. I can draw a circle. But I don't know what you are thinking and my mind won't allow me the freedom to just draw anything because the result has to be what you want. I need to get it right and please you. I have such a busy mind and it's asking:

- How big should the circle be?

- Should I draw in pen or pencil?

- Where should I draw it on the paper?

- Should it be coloured in, shaded or left empty?

- Does it have to be perfect and should I draw around something?

- Why are you asking me to draw a circle?

Give me an instruction that says, 'With a pencil, draw a circle two centimetres in diameter in the centre of a piece of A4 paper. Leave the circle empty and use a pair of compasses and a ruler. We're going to use this to represent the head of a cartoon character.' This I can do! And you are a genius for giving such a clear set of instructions. Your instruction has helped me to see the bigger picture so I don't get stuck in the detail. The purpose and overall reason for a task is something I struggle to comprehend. I prefer things that have precise answers. People with autism tend to struggle with language and comprehension but excel in things like mathematics. It was true for me when I was at school and the only reason I was placed in the third set in mathematics was because I had difficulty comprehending the instruction. I was good with numbers and accuracy but not so good at understanding what to do. I needed longer to process things, so the teacher took more time to explain methods and showed me how to arrive at the answer. I think my son had similar issues because his teacher commented that she noticed that he 'played' with numbers and she tolerated this because she found it fascinating. (By the way, I scored an A in mathematics, so I got there in the end.)

When my children were studying circles in mathematics, I'd ask them what was pi. They always gave the number 3.14. But my question was 'What is pi?' Simply put, it's the number of times the diameter (the width) of a circle will fit around the circumference (outside) of a circle. You see, my question had several valid answers but I wanted my children to understand how pi is derived. I should have asked, 'How is pi derived?'

I am so glad to tell you that what was a hindrance in the past is now a unique gift. My analytical mind works backwards from the result and questions things that others fail to consider, so that the result is even better. I can spot errors and things that aren't supposed to be there, and my mind focusses on outcomes and produces some very interesting solutions to problems. I've learned to give my mind permission to do anything it wants with problem solving, and although what I've learned in the past is useful, it doesn't restrict my thinking or approach. Those maze puzzles that ask which route is the right one to take are great. Have a look at the one below.

Which route will lead to the chequered flag?

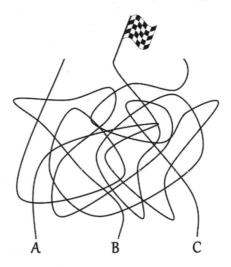

My brain naturally works from the end point backwards. You may call it cheating but your approach may hinder you when looking for solutions by starting at the problem.

Incidentally, neither A, B or C leads to the flag. You probably assumed the answer had to be A, B or C based on your past experience and rules you learned. Yet I never said what the rules were. Try ignoring assumed rules, consider all the possibilities and you will find the answer.

My mind now has the freedom to ignore the rules, visualise the solution and then work backwards. However, I would add one important point here: I need some time to process the problem. And that's true for many children with autism: they need time to process the question a teacher may pose, so a rapid-fire question-and-answer session is not the best environment for them. This approach will mask their true ability, because the more time the pupil is given, the more accurate the answer will be. I was always slower than the rest, but my answers were usually correct and I eventually caught up.

Brainstorming or group work isn't helpful, either. In fact, you might be interested to know that brainstorming sessions, so readily advocated by businesses, can fail to come up with the best ideas because it's the dominant extroverts who push their ideas ahead of the introverts. If you want some good ideas and value every individual, allow the introverts, quiet ones or autistic people time to work through ideas on their own and then ask them privately what they have come up with. You'll be surprised what you could have missed. A good teacher or manager will know how to help each person to contribute because he or she will not assume everyone responds to the same approach with equal enthusiasm.

One last thing. I can remember as a child either being very fixated about how to do things or struggling to accept suggestions from others. I could be very stubborn. That wasn't because I was deliberately disobedient but because my mind was focussed on one method. As my friend once reminded me, we adults need to pick our battles. If it's not vital, why fight? If your child or pupil seems adamant that they are not going to carry out an instruction exactly as you request, it may be because they have another way. Often the best thing you can do is plant a seed, step back and see what happens. Several times my own children have shown indifference to my suggestions. Instead of forcing home my point, I have on occasion just waited and not long after I have seen them doing what I suggested, albeit in a slightly different way. You see, bad behaviour isn't always bad – sometimes it's just behaviour. Choose not to take offence.

Children spend most of their time in school or at home, so I believe the focus needs to be on good relationships between teachers and parents. Both need each other and each has something to contribute to ensure the education path for the child is a little less bumpy. Can I encourage you all to work together, to find common ground and make decisions with the best outcomes in mind? That would be brilliant because children with autism will be consistently inconsistent and they, like all children, cannot behave well all the time. They should not be expected to leave their autism at the door. After all, we wouldn't expect someone who uses a wheelchair to leave it at the school gates and walk in like everyone else. The miracle comes when we change our attitude.

Leaving school was one of the happiest days of my life. I achieved fairly good results and was not sad to leave an inflexible system that caused so much anxiety. However, university was a completely different experience.

Can I help you?

To summarise, then, here are 15 things that would describe me when I was at school:

1. Lacks confidence or continually asks questions about simple tasks.

2. Shy and nervous. Avoids eye contact.

3. Delay in processing questions and doesn't seem to get the 'big picture'.

4. Slow to start or finish tasks, or takes a different approach.

5. An active mind that finds focus somewhat difficult because it processes everything else that's happening.

6. Sensitive to teasing.

7. Few friends and chooses to spend time alone.

8. Doesn't like working in groups and will avoid it if possible or 'fails' to contribute.

9. Always seems to be in trouble and unable to explain events.

10. Fails to apply the rules in every situation, especially the unspoken ones.

11. Does not instinctively know what to do in each situation.

12. Unable to see consequences of actions.

13. Easily taken advantage of by others.

14. Says things out of context or without further explanation.

15. Can be blunt or appear rude.

Are you seeing some of these things in your children, pupils or colleagues? Here are 15 things that might help:

1. Give clearer instructions and remove ambiguity.

2. Avoid brainstorming and rapid-fire questions.

3. Give time to process information and allow them to withdraw to 'reset' their brain.

4. Accept that someone may provide a different answer to a problem either because you didn't explain things clearly or maybe because they've discovered something you haven't seen.

5. Explore events and give time for explanation. Reach conclusions less quickly and only once all the facts are to hand. Accept that you may not have the whole picture.

6. Never shout or make them afraid. Be gentle.

7. Smile and be reassuring. A smile will always increase your face value.

8. Structure and boundaries are comforting. Freedom of choice and decision making can cause stress. Keep the rules simple and avoid grey areas.

9. Consider if group work is essential and, if it is, ensure you facilitate participation. You cannot leave the group to its own dynamic as the extroverts will dominate.

10. Provide some one-to-one time, but don't force eye contact because it's very uncomfortable and can become physically painful. Make sure there's space between you. Forcing eye contact may cause anxiety and distress, and it isn't proof that they are listening to you. The person uses their ears for that.

11. Encourage and praise them. Praising the achievement or how well a task has been done may work better than praising them personally. I liked to be told I'd done a good job rather than be told I was a good boy. It's a subtle difference but it reinforces talents and usefulness when a person is trying to fit in or learn what they're good at. Recognising virtuous qualities at an identity level is great, though – 'You are very honest.'

12. Bullying takes all sorts of forms and the autistic child may be more sensitive to 'minor' things. Nevertheless, take their complaints seriously.

13. Don't take offence too easily. Sometimes what is said is honest observation and he or she may not even understand offence has been caused. Be less hasty to judge. In this politically correct world, autistic people

find conversation a minefield. They do not know the unspoken rules or see the body language around them – you have to tell them. In my home we speak plainly and straight to the point because it helps those of us with autism. Unfortunately, my children's teachers often took offence at the same plain speaking at school, so I quite often had to explain that that was how we communicated at home.

14. When things go wrong, explain why and how to avoid the situation. Bear in mind that the application of rules may be difficult to understand in different situations, so things may go wrong again. Don't keep changing rules or adopt different rules on different days. Be consistent. Oh, and don't be too harsh or exaggerate a problem, but be fair and maintain boundaries. Children with autism will be consistently inconsistent.

15. Believe that you are privileged to meet an exceptionally gifted person and that you may be able to help them use their gift. You can make an amazing difference in their lives as you get to know each child as an individual.

4

University Challenge

> 'A man who has never gone
> to school may steal from a freight
> car; but if he has a university education,
> he may steal the whole railroad.'
>
> *THEODORE ROOSEVELT*

I love deep philosophical sentences. I especially like this one I thought up: 'Life is like a strawberry jelly – you never know which way it's gonna wobble!' You're wondering if it has to be strawberry, aren't you?

░░░░░░░░░░░░

Not long ago my wife and I took the very emotional journey to leave one of our daughters in a city. This was not a punishment or an attempt to see if she had read the story about Hansel and Gretel. Nor was it a way of reducing the weekly food bill. No, this was the day our daughter left home to study at university. I use the term 'to study' in a very abstract and loose way. 'To party' may be a better alternative.

The university is next door to the hospital, which is in turn close to the police station and law courts. Right across the road is a prison – I nearly drove in there thinking it was the campus. It was great to know there were so many local amenities.

I have to report that my daughter appeared to be delighted in her new-found freedom (most baby penguins feel the same until they see a killer whale) and we reluctantly departed. We're glad the nest isn't totally empty of chicks, but it is a strange feeling to see one of them leave. Yet that's the point of all parenting, isn't it? To see our child live as fulfilled a life in the world as he or she is able. As we left, there was another realisation – we've done a good job. In fact, we've done the best job we could to help our daughter to choose to make her own way in life. She may face a few 'killer whales' and leap out of the water, but we're going to encourage her to keep on the path towards independence. Sure, it's tough not seeing her around so much – I keep thinking she's asleep in her room at night. My friend once told me that it's the ones who remain flexible that survive. So we've all got to adjust and go with the change. Life is wobbling.

A big part of university life is the social circle. It's like the magic circle but requires a different set of skills to join. For me, friendship is an illusion with smoke and mirrors. Determining what's real and what's not isn't easy. Like inexperienced magicians whose assistants don't last long after the sawing-in-half trick, in the past my friendships also tended to be short-lived. I liked people. In fact, I loved people. They were just too complex for me to sustain anything lasting. Today I'm comfortable with the strategy of having just a few friends. How many do you need at one time anyway?

I think my daughter is incredibly brave. She's doing what I was ill-equipped to do at her age – leave the safety of home and make new friends out of total strangers. Didn't I spend many years teaching her not to speak to strangers? Time to unlearn a rule.

You may be wondering why I 'failed' to do what my daughter has done. That's an interesting viewpoint when I've never been unemployed, have been married nearly 25 years, have four children, run a small business, am appointed as an IT associate director of a financial services company, advise parents and schools about disability and special needs law, and even have a cycling proficiency badge. (This last one is the most meaningful, particularly as it took me so long to learn to ride a bicycle!)

Failure and success are, I think, quite subjective terms. Who defines success? Who defines failure? Let's go back to the inventor of the light bulb, Thomas Edison. When he was asked what it was like to fail 2500 times before he invented the light bulb, he replied that he never failed. Inventing the light bulb was a 2500-step process. Why? Because despite something not working on the thousandth attempt, each attempt taught him what didn't work and to make some adjustment. It led him ever closer to what he was trying to achieve. I'm glad he didn't give up! We learn more from our 'failures' than our 'successes'.

So perhaps you're now wondering how I've managed to arrive at this point without a university education. Let me say first of all that I've not 'arrived'. I'm still learning and that's key for me. I'm inquisitive and naturally curious about life, and that means I get bored easily. I need to discover new things and apply my mind. I'll never arrive and I like it that way. Second, I did attend university, surviving just short of a month. That 'university challenge' experience has taught me some important lessons that I've carried with me ever since. They can help anyone facing change, and if you're interested, I'll share them with you.

Are you ready for this?

Learn to make decisions for yourself

How hard this is! Especially when you've lived in an environment where you have to ask before you act. If there's one thing I can look back on and remember, it is my inability to make decisions based on what I wanted to do. No one gave me permission to do this and that's the point: I didn't know I didn't need anyone's permission. I was waiting for someone to tell me what to do and I waited a long time. Patience may be a virtue but it can also be an excuse for indecision when a change in direction is needed.

I think it all comes back to unlearning rules. When we're young, we're taught to ask first (at least I was when I wanted a biscuit from the biscuit tin). That's great for a five-year-old but at 18 we really ought to be on the road to figuring things out for ourselves and making our own choices. Why?

Because we shouldn't pass the responsibility of our lives over to someone else. It's not helpful to look back with regrets and blame others for not pursuing your own dreams and creating choice for yourself. My friend would probably ask you, 'So what do you want?'

Being tossed and turned by the influence of others in directions we don't want to go can only make us unhappy. We're not meant to be caged, and we who are parents should remember not to hold on too tight. Our dreams are not their dreams. We have to let our children go and prepare them for life. Otherwise, a white-bearded man wearing sandals, rugged clothes and carrying a staff may turn up from the desert shouting, 'Let my people go!' Have you seen Charlton Heston as Moses? Great film.

Sure, it can be scary making decisions and a little risky too. If you have autism, then it's even harder because we fear the criticism of others and naturally avoid conflict. What will they think? Will they accept me? How do I explain? It's not easy but it's not impossible. Risk is part of the game if you want to be fulfilled. Let me give you a personal example.

When I was 22, I went to stay with a friend in Scotland. We had a great time and I told him that I wanted to get married. He was genuinely pleased for me. Yet there was one problem I shared with him. How would I tell my mother? I didn't know what she'd say and I was nervous. My friend's reply was fairly straightforward, although I was not sure it helped me with a winning strategy. He said, 'Sometimes you just have to take the bull by the horns.'

My mother was no bull, but I knew what he meant. The term had been explained to me before! Sometimes you have to take a risk for something you really want, regardless of what others may say or think. In fact, just before I was going to ask my mother what she thought, she asked me, 'When are you going to get married?' It turned out fine in the end and I needed no cattle prod!

If you want friends, then put yourself in the place where you can be found

Hide and seek is not a good idea. Hide from your enemies but not your friends. Since your life matters and has value to others, don't be a hidden treasure. It's not easy to come out into the open and make friends, but at least decide that your paths will cross with those of others so that you can be discovered.

When I was at university, the biggest mistake I made was to stay in my room. I ended up more isolated and cut off from potential friends. I didn't have a plan for making new pals. It became agony to venture out and I hardly spoke to anyone. I think they guessed I was unhappy, but no one came alongside and helped me. It was this, I believe, that caused me to leave. In my teens there was no diagnosis for Asperger's. You were just shy and withdrawn, a little quirky or just plain weird! But no matter how I tried, the social awkwardness I felt never went away. Even among friends, I felt like a stranger. Imagine then being placed among real strangers – now that was terrifying. I could have done with some help, because in the same way that you're unable read someone's mind, I couldn't read their body language or social cues. Had a diagnosis been available, maybe the university could have ensured I was integrated more easily. That's why I think a diagnosis can be liberating rather than a life sentence. We can understand our vulnerabilities and strengths and know how to make life a little easier so things don't hold us back.

If you're the outgoing type, you can help people with autism. How? It's really simple. When you see someone alone in their early days at college or university, make a point of introducing yourself and inviting them to an event. Tell them you'll take them there and go and get them. You could be the person who makes the difference that will change the course of their life and you may discover a really loyal friend in the process. How great is that?

Be prepared to be vulnerable

'This isn't easy for me.' Can you say that? Admitting you find something hard is liberating for you and others. It allows others the opportunity to help you and return a favour. It enables you to make the first steps towards freedom.

I read a story about two whales that became stuck under the ice in Alaska. It was during an American presidential campaign and for a few days attention shifted from the candidates to the whales. At first a few Eskimos tried to break up the ice with a chainsaw to create some air holes. Their efforts were noticed and marine biologists got involved. However, progress was just too slow. So a gigantic 11-ton ice-breaking Archimedean screw tractor was brought in to churn through the ice. Still with miles to go and increasing media coverage, next to arrive was an Alaska National Guard helicopter armed with a five-ton concrete ice crusher to pound the ice into pieces. Coverage of the event was worldwide by now, and so the Russians turned up with a huge ice-breaker ship. It took great effort and expense but eventually the operation succeeded. Two whales slipped out to sea, much to the delight of their rescuers and the general public.

The point of telling you this story is that quite often people really do want to help you when you get stuck. You just need to let them in by being prepared to be vulnerable.

Discover your talents and believe there's more to come

I guess most of us reassess our lives from time to time and try to work out what to do next. Maybe you've found you're interested in something or have a natural ability in some area but are looking for reassurance to dip your toe in the water and see what it's like. You don't need me to tell you what to do and I wouldn't anyway. You have to work it out for yourself because you need to learn to make your own decisions. It's your life.

However, by way of assistance, let me remind you of something. Pursuing what you're good at makes perfect sense. You need to harness the tremendous motivation that is provided by your special interest and build on what you know is a great place to continue developing your specialism.

And, if you're like me, you'll need to keep learning because you might just get bored sticking at the same thing unless you're having fun. You're allowed to change your mind whenever you want to. How liberating is that!

I've found that my interests and career have naturally changed every five to ten years. One thing has led to another and sometimes I've been taken by surprise by an opportunity I wasn't expecting. Others saw something I hadn't noticed and asked me to give it a go. Most things have worked out well, and although I could stay in the same career or have the same interests, there's more to come. It's what keeps life interesting. I can say, though, that the things that have worked well are those that make use of my strengths. I'm all for trying new ideas and learning to develop strategies to compensate for weaker areas, but your strengths ought to be a point of focus as you discover your talents. We're not meant to all be the same. Let me tell you another story to illustrate this.

A village of woodland animals decided that to meet the challenges of life they ought to set up a school where everyone could be trained. To make things easier, everyone had to take the same lessons in running, climbing, swimming and flying.

The duck was superb at swimming and was even better than his instructor. However, he only made basic grades in flying and was poor at running. Since he was a slow runner, he had to give up swimming lessons and stay late to practise more running. This caused his webbed feet to become sore and he only managed an average score in swimming. But nobody worried about being average except the duck.

The rabbit was top of the class when it came to running but he developed a nervous twitch because of all the extra effort he had to put in to achieve any grade in swimming. His flying abilities were a disappointment to all his teachers, and he became sad and withdrawn.

The squirrel, however, was brilliant at climbing. He would have been good at flying too, except that his teacher made him start from the ground up rather than from the top of the trees which came more naturally to him. All the extra work from having to change the way he did things only led to average climbing and running grades. He excelled in nothing.

The eagle was a problem child. He was severely reprimanded for not conforming to standard practices. In climbing classes he beat everyone to the top of the tree but insisted on using his own way to get there.

The point of the story is this. Every one of us is different and we possess our own natural set of abilities and ways of doing things. It's okay to be you and pursue your own capabilities and style. Don't compare yourself to others all the time – you're unique. You never see a frustrated squirrel trying to be like a duck, do you?

So there you have it. Four tips I have found helpful when facing change. They can be used for any situation, whether that's a new school or college, leaving home or starting a new job. The list is endless because life is like a strawberry jelly – you never know which way it's gonna wobble.

Can I help you?

So, here are my four tips again:

1. Learn to make decisions for yourself.

2. If you want friends, put yourself in the place where you can be found.

3. Be prepared to be vulnerable.

4. Discover your talents and believe there's more to come.

5

I Owe, I Owe, it's Off to Work I Go ...

'Opportunity is missed by most people because it is dressed in overalls and looks like work.'

ATTRIBUTED TO THOMAS EDISON

People ask me sometimes what I do for a living. I reply that my job is very educational. Every night, when I go home, I say, 'Well, that taught me a lesson!'

The world of employment offers challenges to everyone, whether or not they have autism. We all have those 'bad days' and get discouraged. It's probably true that those of us with autism conditions are more prone to anxiety and discouragement, but employment can be very rewarding, provided one rule is followed: find a job that plays to our strengths and at the same time cultivate a hobby that we can develop into a career.

I'll share with you my employment journey because I think it illustrates the struggles I've faced and also the really good things that can happen. I know parents worry about what will happen to their children in the employment arena, and I know there are adults with autism conditions struggling to find work. There are organisations to help young people find work because employers haven't discovered the advantages autism can bring to the workplace.

When I was a child, I'd earn money by taking empty fizzy lemonade Corona bottles to the local newsagents to get back the deposit. I remember searching the woods for bottles to take back so I could buy sweets. The shopkeeper was surprised to see me so often with so many bottles and eventually he began to question my drinking habits.

Summer holidays offered me the opportunity to earn some cash by digging up peat from the local woods. Our garden backed on to a large woodland area and the leaves that fell from the trees created excellent organic peat over the years. My job was to dig up a barrow-load of peat in exchange for ten pence. Back then, ten pence could buy two and a half Mars bars, so my father's rate of pay wasn't too mean. It was, as I remember, back-breaking work, but sometimes I'd manage ten barrows. The council never came to visit my house, although I'm sure today my activities would be classed as illegal. Still, my father wanted the peat for his garden and I wanted the money.

My family wasn't poor, but I was taught the value of money and that sometimes we had to go without until we'd saved up. That's an awfully hard lesson for a child who collected toy cars but a necessary one I've carried with me. I'm not a fan of credit but I've learned that there's good debt and bad debt. Good debt helps to finance things that make more money which can service the debt and have some left over. Bad debt funds a lifestyle with no return. So, wherever possible, I ask myself, 'What will the money return to me?' Borrowing for a car may enable me to go to work to earn a living. Borrowing more for a flashy car may only play to my ego and there's not much reward for that. You have to look after debt; that's called 'servicing'. You can't neglect it or pretend it will go away. So, if you have to take a loan, be sure to look after it and pay the monthly fee.

I remember entering the sacred school careers office. It was usually filled with cigarette smoke – mainly, I think, because the teacher didn't want to see our faces. He wasn't filled with much hope for me.

'Who is it?' came the desperate cry from the careers officer.

'I'm Burns, sir,' I replied.

'Ah, yes. I've got your card here. What do you want to do when you grow up? I've got you down for a train driver just like all the other boys. Is that all right or would you rather I changed it to bus conductor?'

Many at my school could have replied with a list including bank robber or extortionist (I thought the latter was someone who manipulated their body into shapes but later learned that was a contortionist). I replied, 'I'd like to be either a doctor or a comedian.'

'Not much chance of a doctor. You need straight As. And I don't find you very funny, either. Have you considered working with the dead?' was his suggestion.

I was consequently sent on work experience to a nearby hospital's pathology department.

I'd always wanted to be a doctor because I cared about people. I had the noble wish to help people get better because I spent many days in hospital, having been born with a cleft lip. Great Ormond Street Hospital was a welcome vacation for me because I became the centre of attention and everyone was kind to me. I didn't have to try so hard not to make mistakes. People take pity on sick animals and I was no exception!

The comedian side grew from a love of watching Morecambe and Wise shows. I thought they were great and I wanted to make people laugh too. For many years people did laugh at me, but eventually I managed to turn it around to have them laugh at jokes and funny stories. Today I find fun and comedic situations just about anywhere. I see the funny side of things pretty much in every situation. Only the other day I noticed the local town's Easter egg hunt had a strange participant. Families had to take their children around to 29 different shops to find the clue to the Easter quiz. Thing is, one of the participating establishments was a funeral parlour. I could just imagine a child asking why people looked so unhappy or running away screaming, having opened a casket.

My first 'real' job involved working in a wind tunnel, testing roof tiles. I remember arriving for the interview in plenty of time. I was nervous, unprepared and inexperienced. What I had going for me were good A level results. They demonstrated an ability to learn and intelligence to follow instructions. Testing roof tiles was boring, but I honed my woodworking skills under the watchful eye of Eric. He was the team's carpenter and built all sorts of test rigs. I learned to use the right tools for the right job. What I found challenging was being sent on errands to fetch something from another workshop only to be stopped and questioned further by another department head. Unprepared for further questions, I had to return to Eric empty-handed. My natural shyness made interaction somewhat difficult, but I'm grateful Eric took me under his wing and helped me gain confidence. He introduced me to other staff and broke down some of the barriers to make it easier. It was here I also learned to drive a forklift truck, transporting mini skips up and down the hill to be emptied. I enjoyed the responsibility and the freedom of driving the forklift, but I have to admit I got bored easily. I needed a challenge to keep the grey cells working.

After two years of testing roof tiles, driving forklifts and honing my woodwork skills, I applied to work in the local council's planning department. I decided to apply because I knew I'd have to overcome my shyness by meeting the public and answering the telephone. I was determined and I was taken on as a clerk. That was the start of a ten-year career in local government, where I worked in the departments most hated by the public. It helped overcome shyness but not the social awkwardness I felt inside. That has never changed to this day.

The planning department was full of angry people. They were either angry because a planning application had been passed and the uninterrupted view of the countryside from their attic window was going to be spoilt, or their application to build an extension had been refused. It became an art to quickly guess why they were angry and look sympathetic to their cause. I was glad I didn't make the decisions because I could always blame the planning officers. I quickly became the good cop. However, I was occasionally shouted at by members of the public but, in retaliation, I managed to annoy them by saying I got a 50 per cent discount off my rates bill or that the rates helped to pay for the office party (neither was true).

After another two years I transferred to the finance department and worked in the poll tax section. I was enjoying my job interview success, although I should have realised that few people wanted to take the position of a hated bureaucrat. I should have spotted it coming when there were more jobs than applicants. After a year or so of enduring insults (mainly from my manager), I accepted a position in the business rates department. This was great fun. I could lie to the public and no one would ever know. I'd say things like 'Business rates are just a tax to help pay for staff company cars!' and then give a false name. Calls weren't recorded, and I thought if members of the public were allowed to shout at me for things that weren't my fault, then I'd devise ways to annoy them like crazy.

What I liked about the new job was the necessity to learn all the relevant legislation. It became my task to read all the new laws and also update all the rating valuations. It was precise and detailed work, and my boss knew he could rely on me to get everything exactly right. It was perfect. One day I'd be reading law and telephoning a government department to tell them the effect of what had been passed (I was good at finding gaps in the new law) and the next I'd be calculating complex rates bills. I sat examinations and continued to gain qualifications that were relevant to the job and interested me. I became an expert and helped the council save £350,000 off its own rates bills. As my knowledge increased, so did my confidence when helping the public. Conversations were about the things I knew, so I became less fearful.

One of my tasks was to visit all the empty commercial properties to see if anyone was operating a business without informing the council. It was perhaps the one time people were not pleased to see me, so I developed a new tactic. I'd arrive unannounced but act as if I was on their side. I'd take an appeal form and talk about how awful the rates were and that they really ought to appeal. I'd ask if they'd like me to fill out the front half of the appeal form and they'd usually agree. They would then give me their details and the date they'd moved in. I'd then return to the office and generate a bill. Job done! I was managing to be a bureaucrat who was popular, and by learning a few social tactics I avoided being shouted at. The key was to make friends instead of enemies, even if that meant a bit of pretence.

My uncle was the president of an IT training company and I was offered the chance to train in programming. Although I'd resisted IT because most of my family already had that career, I was ready for a new challenge. With some internal staff changes and the merging of the finance and IT sections, I was able to switch allegiances and scoop up some training. This was the start of an IT career that has lasted more than 20 years.

A career in IT generally involves moving around and switching employers. This is something I found quite challenging because I didn't enjoy change and getting to know new people. This isn't unusual, but for people with an autism condition it's even harder. What I learned to do was look back on experiences where change resulted in a positive outcome. I don't think change gets any easier as I get older but the strategy helps. I also found that as my job changed so did the amount of responsibility and freedom to make choices and decisions. Making my own decisions and taking responsibility is something I prefer to being on the receiving end of instructions that have no flexibility. I like to explore options, try out ideas and be a little creative when it comes to problem solving. My analytical skills enable me to look for things that shouldn't be there rather than just test to see if things work as they were designed. My approach helps me to spot what others miss, and I was only able to develop this skill once I had the freedom to choose. Knowing I enjoy the freedom to be creative, I also encourage my colleagues to do the same when time allows. I figure that people prefer to come up with their own solutions rather than have me dictate everything and control what's done. I accept I don't know everything and that managing a team means playing to everyone's strengths and knowledge to get the job done. That's what being part of a team means – fitting the strengths and abilities of different people into various gaps so that together we can achieve the end goal. It's not about everyone needing to be the same. It's about a willingness to share our different talents.

My IT career gave me opportunities to learn how to present ideas and also speak to groups. It's all about pretending to be confident and talking about things we know. Being prepared – by checking equipment, going through slides and practising what to say – is essential. It's something we can learn if we want that type of role. The alternative is to find someone who can present your ideas for you with equal passion and belief.

IT contract work took me into different companies which all faced similar problems. It didn't take long to see the solution, and I think the more we listen in order to understand, the more we learn and the easier it is to see the solution. The social interaction centred on my knowledge and skills, which made it somewhat easier. Keep listening and learning is my advice. Careers in IT, engineering, science or finance suit people with autism conditions – there's plenty to learn and these roles can dovetail with our ability to absorb knowledge and become experts.

Although I've always been comfortable discussing work, social events outside of the workplace, such as office parties or meals, have always proved uncomfortable for me. Social chit-chat and small talk just doesn't come naturally and I find myself silent even though I'd like to contribute. I genuinely like people but I find them a little complicated in the unpredictable social environment.

Employing someone with autism has clear benefits. Sure, you have to be clear with instructions and examine your own communication skills when employing us, but people with autism tend to be very loyal, have less time off for sickness and become experts in the tasks the job attracts. We're the sort of people who, when given the opportunity to learn, soak it in and spot what others miss. We have ideas that can help the business and we genuinely care about doing a good job. We want to please our employer and wouldn't want to take advantage or pilfer. In fact, we can become absorbed in what we do and forget the time and end up working late. Someone who is conscientious and has an attitude of wanting to please should be very employable, provided the employer sees beyond the disability and appreciates the gift. And that leads me to a question I am often asked: 'Should I tell my employer about my autism or reveal it on my job application or at an interview?'

My thoughts on whether you should tell the employer depends on the reason for doing so. If you are being misunderstood or things are not going well because instructions are vague, it may be a good idea to explain. It's not your employer's fault that they don't know about your needs if they are not obvious – you have to tell them. That shouldn't affect your opportunities within the company for promotion, training or any other benefit. What it does do is ensure that your employer considers what reasonable adjustments can be made to accommodate your needs – good employers do want to help. Just as it's not the employer's fault for not knowing, it is not your fault that you have an autism condition. So try to work together for the very best outcome.

The current UK law does support people with autism. When you apply for employment, employers shouldn't ask about your health or any condition before offering you work. I've been reassured that out of all the interviews I've attended, I've never been asked these sorts of questions. Please don't let the fear of an interview stop you applying for a job you're interested in – you might be the very person they need.

My approach has been to always highlight what I'm good at – analysis, problem solving, attention to detail, dedication, loyalty, honesty and integrity. I've never revealed anything else at interview, but my current employer does know about my autism and is very supportive. They recognise my strengths and I'm able to help others in the company with similar conditions. My employer knows that I genuinely care about the business and I carry a huge responsibility for internal IT systems and controls. My straight talking enables colleagues to make decisions with the facts to hand, and I'm encouraged to speak my mind. My contribution is valued and I'm an equal member of the management team. I've no doubt that the positive aspects of autism have enabled me to get things done and make real improvements to the business, and what's important is the outcome.

You have the right to choose whom you tell – isn't choice a wonderful thing? There's no shame in having autism and, as I've previously explained, it has its advantages. You don't have to tell anyone if you don't want to, and if everything is going well, you might not feel the need.

I have to admit I wasn't very good at interviews and perhaps declaring 'why' might have helped. I think I came across as too quiet and reserved, but maybe that's what some employers want if you are going to work in a library or catalogue items in a museum. What I do think is worthwhile is to have practice interviews at college or job support groups. Anything that can help us to be prepared or gain more experience has to be useful if we're not naturally confident with interviews. Having the appropriate skills is not always enough. A good work ethic, positive attitude and willingness to learn are equally important. It may be easy to train someone and alter their skillset, but it's quite another challenge to change their attitude.

My encouragement to you if you are looking for work is to persevere and keep going. It's easy to feel bad when you're unsuccessful, but don't give up. You are of value and just as important as anyone else, and there are people in organisations who want to help you – get in contact with your local council. While you're looking for work, keep yourself busy with reading to learn more, voluntary work or even helping around the house. That way, when you do get an interview, you have something to say when they ask what you are doing at the moment. My friend's wife helps young people and she encourages those between jobs to start a project called 'Project Home'. It's all about finding ways to help out at home and learn skills and develop a positive attitude rather than just watch television. Staying active and cutting the grass or decorating the house at least shows a potential employer that these young people are motivated. It looks great on a job application and can become a talking point.

I said at the beginning of this chapter that we should develop a hobby or interest that can become a career. One reason is that the hobby will probably play to our strengths. It may enable us to take the opportunity to change career path and remain or become employed. For example, I've met many people who enjoy assembling computers at home for friends and family. It doesn't take much to make the transition between having this sort of interest and becoming a self-employed computer Mr Fix-It. So take a look at what interests you and nurture it into something society needs. Since many people with autism conditions struggle with authority, self-employment provides a way of being our own boss.

Someone once told me about her son who loved gardening. He found school difficult but loved being in the garden. He found it peaceful and calming and now runs his own landscaping business. He is very meticulous in his work and the results are brilliant for his customers. He's married, has a son and can afford to buy a house. Maybe this encourages us to see that if the school system doesn't quite work for us, there are other routes. I'd encourage everyone to do their best at school, not least because the education is free. However, the traditional route of gaining qualifications and a job is not the only way. There are apprenticeships and vocational training courses, and developing our own business is possible even when we're young.

Bill Gates' interest in computing began at the age of 13 and he started his first business at 15, earning $20,000. He was very gifted academically and, once he had been moved to a new school, did well in most subjects. Although he enrolled at Harvard to study law, he left after two years to pursue a business career in IT. In 1975, at the age of 20, he and a friend, Paul Allen, started Microsoft. If you read about Bill Gates, you'll see quite a few journalists believe he has Asperger's. Regardless of that, Bill Gates has used his strengths to start with nothing and create a global company. And that's my point: learn what your strengths are and lean towards them. It's not about becoming famous; it's about using what you have to develop a career you enjoy. What do you need to get to where you want to be? Start building a plan, keep learning and remain flexible. That way you'll be better prepared to take opportunities that come to you. Sometimes there are no rules or guarantees. It can be about discovering what works well for you, so don't get upset when others have a clear sense of what they want to do and you don't. Many people still change careers later in life.

You may be wondering if I have a hobby or interest at the moment. I have to admit my interests do change, but when I find something, I become absorbed in it. Right now I have a passion for social law and its application in schools for children with disabilities that affect their behaviour. Reading law satisfies my need for complexity and a challenge to my brain. It prevents boredom and keeps the grey cells working. It is quite strange that I seem to be able to grasp the interpretation and application of the law. It has led me to help families and schools and advise them about situations where a child is either not receiving the help they need or has been excluded. Sadly, many school exclusions for continued disruptive behaviour break the law because the behaviour has not been managed by the school through the introduction of reasonable adjustments and an understanding of the child's disability. Reasonable adjustments are meant to enable the child not to be disadvantaged by, for example, a stressful environment or how teachers engage with them. They help to put the child on a more even footing with other pupils.

Most of the cases I review involve those with autism spectrum conditions. I'm well aware of the law and the child's rights and the needs of the other children. However, for me it's about getting the best outcome to prevent exclusions and manage the situation. Education is important, so I work towards helping parents, schools and local education authorities to come together and find the best solution for the child and their classmates. Whatever can be done at the earliest stage can help the child to have a brighter future. Dropping out of education is a slippery slope to problems in teenage and adult years. 'Speak softly and carry a big stick' was President Roosevelt's advice. Knowledge of the law and reading legislation comes naturally to me, and this is the big stick I can carry. Speaking softly is all about building relationships and working towards an outcome everyone can be pleased about. For me, compromise is allowed if an outcome can be achieved that will give the child the best opportunity to receive an appropriate education. Vengeance when things go wrong will only exhaust parents and not bring any lasting benefit for the child. However, I am keen to help schools to learn from mistakes so that future situations can be handled in a way that takes everything into account during any decision that affects the child's future.

I don't know where my interest may lead me, but my experience illustrates how I've been lucky enough to be employed at something that I'm naturally good at and have an interest in, and that helps others. What are you good at? What do you enjoy? Where does your interest lie and where does your inquisitiveness take you?

Can I help you?

Let me end this chapter by reminding you of the strategies that have helped me and I hope will help others too.

- Recognise what you're good at and where your strengths and advantages lie. Head that way when looking for training or employment.

- Start making a plan but remain flexible.

- Persevere and keep going. Find something to do and be useful between jobs.

- There are many different ways to earn a living. Consider which suits you best – whether it's traditional employment, running your own business or an apprenticeship.

- Look for work that will help you become more confident around people.

- Attitude can be more important than knowledge.

- Don't worry if your career is a bit varied because you're unsure what to do. Nothing is wasted and one thing will lead you to another. There's no hard and fast rule – just do your best.

- Develop a hobby or interest that might one day develop into a career.

- Keep learning. Taking a job that's not quite what you want will give you an opportunity to learn and understand something new that might be useful later.

- If school wasn't a great place and you have few qualifications, consider going to evening classes to obtain what you need. Education doesn't end just because we've left school.

6

The Social Calendar

'Courage is being scared to
death ... and saddling up anyway.'

JOHN WAYNE

I was once invited to a wedding. It was a beautiful day
and as I approached the church I was greeted by the
usher with the words, 'Bride or groom?'

'I'm not the groom and I'm sure I don't look like the
bride. I'm a guest, you idiot!'

The social calendar for me is best left unfilled. I don't mean
to sound miserable (my wife would say I am) but I find the
whole experience more challenging than an elephant walking
a tightrope across Niagara Falls. It's quite tricky, every step is
no less risky than the previous one and it looks kind of scary

too. It would be easier never to set out on the journey. But where's the exhilaration or fun in that? I know I'd rather keep the calendar clear, but that's not practical or fair to my family. And perhaps there's a fun time I've not yet experienced.

You see, I love people. I find them fascinating, which is not a good chat-up line, I know. Never go up to a girl and say, 'Hello, you look really fascinating tonight.'

I can be so distracted by the sounds and sights, the detail and events that I easily miss the social interaction bits. Social events can become a study in people rather than an interaction. That then sets me apart from everyone else. They're all having a great time while I write an essay in my mind. When people are flirting, I just think they're being nice to each other. It happens at parties – and am I glad I'm married and don't have to worry about that anymore! But it does mean I have to work out who doesn't want to be interrupted and who's generally having a conversation that anyone can join.

I usually end up on my own at social events unless my wife's around. She doesn't leave me alone too long and she's my rescuer in the sea of people. Many people have the notion, probably from something they've read, that people with Asperger's or high-functioning autism don't want to interact. I'd like to challenge that view because it's not true for everyone. If you think I'm on the outside *looking* in, then you might be missing something quite important, because although I like to watch people, I'm often on the outside trying to *get* in. Let me explain.

When you meet a group of strangers, you may feel awkward at first; then, as you get to know them, you feel a little more relaxed. If these people become your friends, then the next time you meet them it's much easier to join the group. It's not like that for me. Even if I know the people, the awkwardness I feel inside does not go away or subside or decrease in intensity. If I manage to join a group and then move away, I find it difficult to get back in. It's like meeting strangers every time. The question is 'Why?'

I'm sure there are a great many experts who have views and opinions, but these don't really help me. I think the reason is that there's a missing connection, which means that I cannot see social cues. This leads me to question who my friends are and whether someone really does want to talk to me at a party. It's not a lack of confidence or self-worth. I'm looking for a signal like a traffic light. All I'm seeing is the red stop light. There's the odd bit of amber but never green. So I don't know if it's okay to go over and join in. I'm more comfortable if someone comes to me. That doesn't always work, however, because I may be giving out social signals that I'm unaware of that keep people away.

So what's the answer? Two things come to mind. First, I've had to decide to take a few risks by going over. That is quite a hard thing to do in a social setting. Second, I need others to be the green traffic light. A beckoning hand gesture or verbal invite is perfect. That's where others come in. To those of you on the 'normal spectrum', if you know someone struggles socially, be generous with your friends and share them around. Introduce them to the one who's struggling or invite them over to join your group. You won't believe how helpful that is and how much anxiety you can relieve. You might even discover that the person struggling socially has some hidden qualities such as a great sense of humour. I heard of one young man with Asperger's who only liked attending social events that he knew about well in advance so that he could prepare himself. Although he was nervous, everyone there loved him because he'd learned some magic tricks and had brilliant sleight of hand. He brought entertainment and felt comfortable showing his talent.

There's another clue for those of us who struggle in the social scene: if we have a talent, we could learn a routine to share at an event. People love magic. Worth a try, isn't it? I think finding a way of being comfortable in unfamiliar surroundings is key here, and preparation helps. It doesn't have to involve cold clinical planning, but if that helps us to feel safe, then why not? There are no rules: the objective is to be part of the social gathering for as long as we choose. It can be exhausting and you'll enjoy your own space afterwards, but it's worth it, not least because you will be supporting your family or expanding your experience. You don't have to party every night!

So how do I feel comfortable? Well, I haven't quite got there yet, but I have developed some strategies that at least enable me to relax for some of the time. I recognise that there's a side of me that wants to withdraw, but I've begun to decide when that's going to happen rather than do it as soon as I feel I want to. That way I still fully embrace my need for some down time and isolation without letting it completely control me. I don't want anything to prevent me choosing to socialise because I know that people are an essential ingredient in life. Although isolation and socialising seem complete opposites, both are important. The down time

I have enables me to recuperate and de-stress from all the processing my mind undertakes. Without it I'd become very unhappy. It's very tiring for me to socialise, but I really need to because it brings balance to my life.

Going to an event with someone who cares about you is a great idea. I find this really helps because they know what I struggle with and ensure I'm not alone for too long. They can also introduce me to people, be my companion and help me when things are getting a little tricky. They can keep the conversation going along the right tracks and I can contribute as I choose. In contrast, I'm more comfortable with meetings at work because I know the subject matter and can prepare. I do still have to work out when it's my turn to speak, but the boss knows me well and makes an opening for me. He values my contribution and I value his support. Social occasions, however, offer little chance for preparation because you don't know what you'll be asked. That's where your friend can help.

What else do I struggle with?

At social events my hands are two of the things I am very conscious about. Strange, isn't it? It's not that they grow bigger or change colour; it's just that I'm not sure what to do with them. I can't leave them at home, and nobody told me what I could do to feel comfortable until recently. A chance conversation with my aunt taught me something I wish I'd been shown years ago. It's so simple I think it borders on genius. Know what it is? Pick up a glass or a leaflet. Put something in your hand. Carry something. Put your hands to work and then you won't worry about where they should be because they're doing what they need to do. As soon as I arrive at a social event I'm looking for a drink or a plate or a leaflet. I never put it down unless I can replace it with something else. It really works and makes me less anxious. This one simple thing has made a huge difference to how I feel. If I'm at an event at work, one of the things I'll do is take my camera. Something to hold and useful to have rather than become self-conscious. The only issue people have with me being the photographer is I begin to act a bit 'camp'. I once inappropriately said to one of the directors, 'Hello, sweetie. Let me take a photo of you.' He was taken by surprise but saw the funny side.

That leads me on to another strategy at social events – acting and playing the part. I'm not suggesting you can't be yourself, but this is a strategy I use sometimes to engage with others. It's one of the tools I have at my disposal. You see, I like watching films because the interaction between people is usually exaggerated. It's more obvious to see if someone is fond of someone else when you're an onlooker. I guess that's why I like 'people watching'. What I learn from films helps me to interact with others. I've a great deal still to learn but it has helped. If I feel nervous, I imagine what a confident person looks like, how they stand and what they might say. I then copy this and it helps to reduce nervousness.

My wife has an old-fashioned sweet shop in Worthing in Sussex. Quite often I go and help serve the customers and I am at ease interacting. The secret to this is playing a part. I act out a comedy character based on a sketch from the comedy series *The Two Ronnies*. I dress up and have fun. The repertoire may be repeated, and you may say that I'm hiding behind a mask, but I enjoy it because it enables me to be around others in a less formal environment and to do something I feel confident about. I can talk about the history of sweets or tell a few jokes. I'm focussing on what I'm good at – and that leads me nicely on to my next tip.

When you're at a social event, try to find someone with a common interest. If you can't find anyone, ask someone to introduce you to a person with a particular interest. If this happens, you'll be able to talk about things you feel comfortable with and enjoy the other person's contribution. The key here, though, is to know when to stop talking! At what point do you become boring or tedious? Worrying about this could prevent me from ever starting a conversation, but there are one or two things that give me clues so I can let the person go.

If the person glances away, it's my cue to end the conversation. You've got be observant, though. Yawning is another one – if you observe this, then you've probably gone a long way down the tedious road. I quite often look at people's feet. No, it's not some kind of fetish! I glance down to see the direction they are pointing in. If they point at me, then I know they have time to speak with me or are interested. If they point away, I need to let them go.

Breaking off the conversation can be as easy as offering to get them a drink – 'Anyway, I talk too much. Can I get you a drink?' It changes momentum and direction and gives you something to do so either of you can leave. While you get them a drink, they'll usually find someone else to talk to. You can then pass them the drink, smile and move on without any embarrassment. Don't feel rejected – social events are usually all about short conversations and an opportunity to meet. So keep it simple and focus on the other person by asking questions about them (but don't interrogate them). If someone asks you about your job or interests, be sure to ask the same question back because they probably want to tell you all about theirs. People love talking about themselves!

I was at a wedding not long ago and was seated with complete strangers. My wife was sitting opposite so we couldn't talk together so easily, and I was a little stuck about what to say when people went on about their important jobs. I think some people would use the phrase 'up their own arse' to describe them. Well, someone eventually asked me what my job was. I was tempted to reply incorporating the words 'stripper' or 'male prostitute', but since my wife was opposite I thought I had better behave. But nor did I want to reply that I was an associate director for a financial services company. That would sound just like them and too grand for me. Nope. I said, 'I work in a sweet shop.' The conversation changed immediately as people forgot about their 'importance' and became children again. The subject of old-fashioned sweets, fudge, chocolate and bonbons went right around the table. It was much more interesting and something I could join in with because it was a topic I knew about. That's another tip: find something everyone loves to talk about and introduce it somehow.

One of the things it took me a long time to realise is that eating out isn't about the meal. Can you believe that? Going out specifically to buy a meal is all about something entirely different. Nobody ever told me that! I thought that at every meal you sat down, ate and then left. But, then, I don't appreciate requirements based on unspoken rules. If it's unspoken or unconscious, how would I have known? As

I've got older, I've learned. My wife has certainly ensured I stop making the same mistakes – anniversary meals are not the times to rush off to watch television or read a book! So what's eating out all about? It's about interacting. It's about time together. It's about enjoying each other's company. It's about catching up on what's been happening in each other's lives around the pleasant experience of a great meal. Sure, the meal is important – I wouldn't dare take my wife to a fast-food chain on a special occasion. I might not mind, but she would make her feelings known to me in no uncertain terms. In any case, the occasion is about 'us'. The words 'we', 'us' and 'together' replace the words 'I', 'me' and 'alone'. If the meal is important, the person you're sharing the occasion with is even more important. I try to remember that, but I have to admit my mind wanders and I get impatient. I'm a work in progress.

They say, 'If you want to make friends, then you need to smile and give eye contact.' What some people don't realise is people with autistic conditions can find it quite difficult to develop a natural smile. I heard of one guy who deliberately practised smiling but could only manage something that looked creepy or suggestive. It didn't attract the right sort of people! Furthermore, eye contact can not only be uncomfortable but it can become physically painful. Interestingly, in some cultures direct eye contact is actively discouraged and is considered rude or aggressive. In the West, what people take for granted and others insist on having creates a huge hurdle, but I've found an answer to these dilemmas.

First, practise laughing out loud. Watch a comedy, listen to some jokes or read something hilarious. Many say people with Asperger's do not have a sense of humour. I disagree. There is a sense of humour, but for each one it is different. Kind of like everyone else, really. Some like slapstick, some like word play and others like sarcasm. The difference is that a sense of humour might not be so audible for others to detect it. So I advocate learning to laugh out loud. That will help you to smile more naturally.

Second, since eye contact can be uncomfortable, don't do it. 'What?' I hear the experts ask incredulously. You read my words correctly. My strategy is this: do what you're comfortable with and then push the boundaries a little more into the unknown. Maintain some distance, because the closer you are, the more uncomfortable eye contact becomes. Looking towards a person from a distance is more bearable than looking into their eyes from three feet away. So, when you move in closer, start by looking at chins or foreheads. Try looking at ears. Then when you're ready, try looking at noses. Once you've mastered noses, you may choose to glance at eyes and then look away. I bet people won't know whether eye or nose contact is being given.

The last thing I want to share on this subject is honesty. It's a wonderful virtue and to be admired in most situations. However, in the social setting we can be almost too honest. How come? When someone asks how you are, it's not the same as when you visit the doctor. Your doctor wants to know your symptoms, whether you've opened your bowels and what you've been coughing up. That doesn't really apply when you're at a party, social gathering or enjoying a meal with a friend. The fact that you may have been up all night running to the toilet is not going to make a good topic of conversation if you're having a curry. What people say and what they actually mean can be different. It would be helpful if they spoke in a straightforward manner, but that ain't gonna happen!

Being economical with the truth and sparing people the details is a general principle we might like to learn when we're socialising. I'm not saying we should ever lie – just say less. If you have a friend you trust, perhaps you could act out some situations. Actually, this is a great source of comedy – watch comedians on television and you'll see they either exaggerate a situation or take something literally and turn it into something funny. Here's an extract from *The Sweet Shop Diaries* by Walter Jones:

> The annual school trip to London Zoo holds great memories, not least because the most popular kid in the class was so travel sick that he'd spend most of the journey throwing up into a bag. Of course, no one wanted to sit next to him on the coach. As a result, my popularity was briefly elevated. I used to bring bags of sweets from my grandad's sweet emporium. You name it, I had it. Sherbet pips, fizzers, pick and mix, cola cubes, chewing nuts and black jacks were all packed inside my tiny brown leather satchel between the obligatory sandwiches, crisps and drink. I was generous too. I'd share them with all the other kids at very reasonable prices.

Now, at my school we had a trainee teacher called Mr Alfie Evans. We called him 'A & E' for short, as he was a walking casualty.

Since he was pretty useless at most things, I guess that's why he decided to try his hand at teaching kids who might not notice his inadequacies. But he underestimated us. Boy, was he hemmed in by his own incompetence.

I frequently ended up in his group. It was kind of a 'baptism of fire' for him because if he could survive with me for the day, then the other teachers thought he'd probably make it past Christmas.

Alfie Evans would take me and a few other misfits around the zoo and pretend to be knowledgeable. As you'd expect, we were not too interested in his talks. We were more interested in whether we could get the ostriches to eat bubble gum balls.

MR EVANS: Boys, there's a baby elephant.

WALTER: Oh really? I thought that was a penguin.

MR EVANS: No, I think you can tell by the trunk and flappy ears. Yes, it's an elephant. It says so here.

WALTER: Is it an African elephant or an Indian elephant?

MR EVANS: I don't know. Let me read this information board. No, it was born here so I guess he's British.

WALTER: I don't like zoos anyway.

MR EVANS: Why not?

WALTER: I think the animals should be free and not kept in cages.

MR EVANS: Well, they can't just let them out because there are all these people here. They have to keep them locked up in case they hurt someone.

Most of us were not excited about elephants. We'd seen photos and television programmes and we knew you couldn't pick one up. What we loved was Pet's Corner. Let's face it, no one makes a documentary about gerbils or hamsters.

Pet's Corner gave us the opportunity to torment something that couldn't get away or put up a fight. We didn't mean to torment them but, after a day of continuous feeding, I guess you'd feel tormented if you had more food shoved into your mouth.

We all got to hold overweight, cute and furry things or feed baby goats and usually someone would try and smuggle something on to the coach. In those days we got searched, not for cigarettes or drugs but for rabbits, hamsters or guinea pigs. Sometimes the occasional concealed duck would give itself away as we drove out of the car park. Those were great days.

Fast forward now, some twenty years. I'm on a train with my son and several bags of traditional sweets, travelling to London Zoo. He's just four and a half and is naturally curious because he's never been on a train.

I'm thinking to myself, 'I hope he doesn't say anything to embarrass me. He blurts out so much rubbish.'

At that moment, a lady opposite leans over and starts talking to him.

What is it about women and small kids? Why do they have to talk to them? They don't feel the compulsion to talk to me – just kids. If you're a woman be warned by what happened next. Think twice before engaging in conversation with small children.

LADY: Hello, Little Boy. Where are you going today?

WALTER: [Muttering] Oh, no. Don't talk to him. He'll go on aimlessly for the whole journey because he thinks you want to be friends.

SON: London Zoo. I haven't been naughty. We're going to see the animals.

LADY: How lovely. Are you excited?

SON: [To Walter] Daddy, why is this lady so fat?

WALTER: I don't know. Why don't you ask her yourself? I don't want to get involved. I'm getting off at the next stop.

SON: [To Lady] Why are you so fat? Do you eat a lot? My daddy says people are fat because they are pigs.

WALTER: [To Lady] I'm so sorry. He doesn't mean to be rude. He doesn't always know what he's saying.

SON: I do! She's fat and I want to know if she's a pig!

We never went on a train again.

Perhaps one final piece of advice on this topic. I think it is worth remembering not to take things too seriously. The social calendar is not meant to be like a rigorous series of tests set by a tough examination board that we must pass to a high standard. In fact, the social calendar offers us an opportunity to explore and discover new friends as we choose. There's no compulsion. We have a choice and I'd like to encourage you to exercise yours. Instead of staying in and becoming the 'autistic label' people imagine you to be, allow yourself to make decisions to go out and experience life. And as my friend would say, 'What might that be like?'

Can I help you?

To summarise then, here are my tips for social occasions:

- Decide to take a few risks by going over to join in.

- Go to an event with someone who cares about you.

- Develop a talent or party piece.

- Put your hands to work by picking up a glass, plate or leaflet.

- Find someone with a common interest.

- Practise laughing out loud.

- Keep it simple and focus on the other person by asking questions about them.

- Maintain some distance and practise looking at anything except eyes.

- There are no rules – the objective is to be part of the social gathering for as long as we choose.

- Find something everyone loves to talk about and introduce it somehow.

- Try acting and playing a part.

- Be economical with the truth and spare people the details.

- Don't take things too seriously.

7

A Shot in the Dark

'The single biggest
problem in communication
is the illusion that it has taken place.'

*ATTRIBUTED TO GEORGE
BERNARD SHAW*

It was summer and I was on the island of Majorca with my son. A blonde, blue-eyed girl turned to me and asked, 'Would you like a free shot?' Confused, I wondered what she wanted me to shoot at.

I had been recommended an '80s' bar, although I'd protested that I was only 42 and didn't want to enter an establishment frequented by old ladies. It soon dawned on me the term referred to the music and not the clientele. I was totally caught off guard by the barmaid's question because bars were not a place I frequently visited at home. She stared at me for some time and I heard other women start to giggle. Was it so obvious I was out of my depth? To save further embarrassment, I nodded and she produced a small glass of green liquid. I don't remember what she called it, but it wasn't limeade. Although my father worked for a rum merchant, I've never learned how to drink alcohol socially. Most people I'd seen drink had become so drunk that I didn't think that was much fun. I'd never had the inclination to join in.

One of the women who had been giggling came over and the following conversation ensued.

WOMAN: Hello.

ME: Hello.

WOMAN: Are you on your own?

ME: Yes.

WOMAN: Why are you on your own?

ME: I'm on holiday and my son has gone to another club. I thought I'd risk coming in here.

WOMAN: Does he live with you, then?

ME: Yes.

WOMAN: That's nice. I like it when children come to live with their parents. How long has he lived with you?

ME: Since he was born.

It had not occurred to me that she probably thought I was sad and single or divorced. Nor did I detect any form of chat-up line from her. In any case, it wouldn't have worked as I am happily married, have four children (all have lived with me since birth!) and miss pretty much all social cues. Flirting has never been my area of expertise – I tend to think people are just being nice. Some advice here: if you fancy someone, it might be a good idea to just say so if they're not responding to your advances.

I've had many instances where I've made mistakes and misunderstood what someone has said, missing the context. Looking back, I think it's quite funny really. The common element running through all these happenings tends to be the unfamiliar situation.

Some years ago I was on the island of Madeira. Some of you may be asking whether I am the real idiot abroad! These things don't happen to me just because I'm abroad. I manage quite well at home too! Anyway, on one particular day I had turned up at a skateboard shop at the request of my son to purchase some parts for his skateboard. The shop was closed and a young man across the street said he'd let the owner know I was waiting.

I meandered down the old street and came to a building with a sign that said 'Pub'. A lady was standing outside and gestured to me to come in. She was very friendly, like most people on the island. Once inside, I sat on a stool at the bar and it occurred to me that there weren't many drinks on the shelves as you'd find in the UK. Still, this was Madeira. Perhaps they only sold a few of the local favourites. The lady who had beckoned me in then walked behind the bar and the following conversation began:

WOMAN: What can I get you?

ME: Can I have some Coke?

WOMAN: Pardon?

ME: Can I have some Coke?

WOMAN: You want coke?

ME: Yes, please, if it's not too much trouble?

WOMAN: One moment.

The woman went to speak to one of the men in the pub and then came back.

WOMAN: Are you sure you want coke?

ME: Yes, please. A nice cold glass of Coke.

WOMAN: One moment while I get some.

She left the pub and I wondered why she didn't have any Coke in stock. I should have asked for lemonade.

While she was gone, I looked around. It was unusually dark for a pub at noon and it wasn't very busy. I smiled at a girl along the bar who winked at me. She was with her grandfather, I think. She then kept blowing kisses at me and I thought that was quite strange. I was in my shorts, but my legs rarely see daylight and are not that alluring. This was a strange pub indeed. Everyone seemed so friendly, but I felt a bit out of place. The woman returned.

WOMAN: Here, I've got you some Coca-Cola.

ME: Thank you.

WOMAN: Do you want ice?

ME: No, thank you. I can see it's been in the fridge.

WOMAN: You're not from round here are you? Are you on holiday?

ME: How did you guess?

WOMAN: Why did you come in here?

ME: I'm just waiting for the skateboard shop at the other end of the street to open.

WOMAN: Are you looking for company?

ME: Not really. I like being on my own.

WOMAN: What's the matter? Don't you like me?

It was at this point the penny dropped and I realised this pub was not what I thought it was. There were other things for sale that were not on the shelf. I finished my drink as quickly as possible, paid and left. I walked back up the street and met the man I'd previously spoken to outside the shop.

ME: I've just been in that pub at the end of the street and it's not a pub.

YOUNG MAN: No, it's for girls.

ME: I know!

YOUNG MAN: What happened?

ME: I asked for some Coke and they did look at me a bit strange.

YOUNG MAN: You asked for coke?

ME: Yes.

YOUNG MAN: They will have thought you wanted cocaine. Never ask for coke.

ME: Oh dear.

Just then the lady from the pub went into a bar opposite us, looked at me and then spoke to the barman.

ME: That's the lady from the pub!

YOUNG MAN: Yes, she works there.

ME: What's she saying?

YOUNG MAN: She says you visited her bar.

ME: Yes?

YOUNG MAN: And she says she was very disappointed!

Taking a naive trip into unfamiliar territory is like a shot in the dark and I'm never sure what will happen. For some people, that can be very stressful and worrying. Did I tell you autistic people have a greater tendency to worry? They find unfamiliar things challenging, and children especially can become quite upset unless they are prepared in advance.

It's not just situations and instructions I get wrong. Emails and letters offer just as big a challenge because there's little opportunity to ask for clarification. But equally I am less offended by the written word because I don't pick up any underlying tone. It's black and white to me. I think that's one of the broken connections with communication. The context and emotional attachment can be missed, which can lead to an unintentional misunderstanding. If you're asking a question, it's better to say what you mean and ask the question that gives you the information you need. For example, if you wanted to know if I liked cats, you should ask me that exact question. Don't make assumptions. Asking another question such as 'Do you have a pet cat?' would not necessarily mean I don't like cats if I don't own one. Similarly, having a pet cat doesn't mean I like them. Maybe I inherited one. That's where the autistic mind differs. We cannot always see the real question being asked, in the same way that we cannot tell if someone is deceiving us. When it comes to science and research, the autistic mind can be put to good use – exact and quantifiable things are perfect. But social situations aren't like that, and I've found a helpful aid is to reply to an uncertain enquiry with another question: 'What are you actually trying to ask me?'

Changing subjects can also produce interesting responses. I've experienced many occasions when the subject has changed or moved on and I'm still thinking about the previous conversation. I sometimes end up answering the question before last. If you've ever seen *The Two Ronnies'* *Mastermind* sketch where Ronnie Corbett's specialist subject is answering the question before last, you'll know what I mean.

It's possible to understand, then, that people on the autistic spectrum can end up in all sorts of trouble throughout school or with the law during adolescence and adulthood, because we fail to see the underlying question or naively walk into a situation. I remember reading about a case in which a young man was arrested following an incident. The policeman had asked if he had been involved and he said that he had. It turned out he had misunderstood the question because he thought that being a witness to the incident counted as being 'involved'. He also wanted to make sure he gave the policeman the answer the policeman might like to hear. I'm glad there are some police forces being trained in questioning people with autism and I hope this will continue. It's important not to take answers at face value or phrase things in such a way that someone may answer based on what they think you'd like to hear.

I want to conclude this chapter by saying that many people misunderstand situations or statements others make or write. Just try following wardrobe assembly instructions and you will see what I mean. I also want to say that most misunderstandings don't have to be serious if we give each other room to explain and ask questions that are open and make the context obvious. In contrast to the usual phrase, it's not *the way* that you say it but *what you say* that matters.

Can I help you?

Here are some pointers to help everyone when asking questions:

- Say what you mean and be direct.

- Try to include the context in your question, especially if you have recently changed the subject.

- Give the person time to process your questions and allow them room to answer.

- Don't interrupt their answer – it will frustrate and cause them to lose track.

- Choose not to be offended or upset if the answer appears blunt, uncaring or undiplomatic. They are at least trying to answer your question and probably don't mean to offend you.

8

The Escape Plan

'You don't learn to walk
by following rules. You learn by
doing, and by falling over.'
RICHARD BRANSON

I love the story about the man who tried to take his dog to obedience classes but the dog refused to go. I can picture the dog either growling or pushing down with all four paws against being dragged away.

Although I'm not sure we should model our lives on that dog, sometimes learning to refuse to do something or take a stand against something takes real courage. Yet learning the difference between being stubborn or courageous is tricky too. Albert Einstein is supposed to have once said, 'There are two types of people that never amount to much in this world.

Those that can never do what they are told and those that can only do what they are told.'

Elsewhere I've mentioned the importance of unlearning certain rules. It's not that they are bad or wrong, but sometimes they become inappropriate or hindrances in a social situation or in daily life. In fact, rules quite often change from one century to another or within cultures. What's considered polite in the West can be quite rude in Asia. So sometimes rules are subjective. Help!

A person with autism, like myself, has to learn how to live free. Rules we learned or had imposed on us as children can become cages and so an escape plan has to be drawn up to lead us to freedom. In fact, people with autism are the ones who want to ask, 'Why?' Yet they often lack the courage or feel they don't have permission to challenge ideas. I believe it's really important to challenge ideas because that ability is what drives innovation and discovery.

I want to take some common rules and illustrate why they need to be altered or dropped from the list as we get older and how I've managed it over the last two decades. These are social rules as opposed to those that can lead to criminal proceedings when broken!

Take a look at these.

Never talk to strangers

Consider the rule 'Never talk to strangers'. It sounds like perfect sense until you consider flying. Getting on a plane with 300 or so complete strangers and entrusting your life to a pilot you've never met has to be wrong, doesn't it? The air stewards may carry out a safety demonstration but can I really trust them? When they serve the meals, the food could be out of date or maybe they've added a laxative? That's the other thing – meals on planes. You have to eat with complete strangers. I never go out for a meal with complete strangers, let alone sit next to them! When you arrive at your destination and make your way through passport control, you are again confronted by a complete stranger who wants to ask personal questions …

PASSPORT OFFICER: Are you travelling alone?

ME: I'm not saying. I don't know who you are and my mother says I shouldn't talk to strangers.

PASSPORT OFFICER: You have to answer my questions.

ME: Why?

PASSPORT OFFICER: Because there's a security guard over there with a very large truncheon and who knows what he'll do with it if I call him over.

ME: I'm alone. And I don't want a date with you.

PASSPORT OFFICER: Are you here on 'business' or 'pleasure'?

ME: I'm going to see my mother-in-law so I'll let you decide.

PASSPORT OFFICER: I'll assume 'pleasure'.

ME: It's not her funeral.

PASSPORT OFFICER: Where are you staying?

ME: I'm definitely not telling you that!

PASSPORT OFFICER: Guard!

You see, not talking to strangers is not a black-and-white rule. However, a person with autism may find it hard to apply the rule in different circumstances or take a very literal approach to apply the rule in all situations. Spouses and friends can help here. My wife is good at warning me about unsavoury characters, because I'm otherwise too trusting and have learned to talk to anyone rather than no one. That's the risk here: unlearning this rule can put us in a position where we talk to anyone without realising their intentions. We're vulnerable. I've seen others end up in trouble because they were manipulated without realising it. We're not very good at spotting deceit. The trick is to learn to be polite and engage with others while at the same time holding fast to good principles and integrity. The risk is worth it.

Sit up straight at the table

Ever struggled with this one? I remember trying to sit up straight at the table and holding my arms straight out to reach the food in front of me. I'm sure there was an easier way. I get the idea behind the rule but it makes someone look stupid in a restaurant. Take a 34-year-old who sits bolt upright at a table in a restaurant. It makes him stand out and draws unnecessary attention. A situation like this happened to me some time ago. I was at a family meal and we'd invited someone else who happened to have Asperger's. The thing was, he sat bolt upright at the table because he had been brought up that way. It wasn't his fault – no one had shown him what to do, so I figured he needed a little help. I suggested he leaned on the table and slouched a little because the meal was about being together and sharing rather than just eating food. Although he had been brought up with a rule, I said to him, 'I give you permission to put you elbows on the table and lean.' I then led by example and by the end of the evening I had him resemble the Tower of Pisa rather than Nelson's Column. Now there's a useful hint: don't just tell someone what to do – show them and lead by example.

Don't interrupt

My friend has a much better strategy which he taught me. I've found it invaluable. He says, 'Look for the gap and jump in.' I've got to tell you that has to be one of the most helpful things I've learned for social events and work meetings. When I was younger, I could stand around for ages waiting for a conversation to end. I felt ignored and undervalued, but that wasn't the case – I just needed to jump in once I found the gap. Don't just stand there, do something.

Don't lie

Oh boy! Isn't this a tricky walk across a minefield while blindfolded? Being truthful is a characteristic that we admire and promote. After all, what would it be like if politicians could just say what they think and be 100 per cent truthful? The balance between being truthful and withholding the truth is called diplomacy. Some say withholding the truth is the same as lying or being deceitful, but I'd say you need to be married to really understand. No, marriage is not founded on lying or deceit (well, not the last time I looked anyway), but consider the following conversation ...

WIFE: Darling, could you help me?

HUSBAND: Why?

WIFE: I want your thoughts on something.

HUSBAND: I guess I can do that.

WIFE: Now I want you to be honest.

HUSBAND: Ah, okay.

WIFE: Does this dress make me look fat?

HUSBAND: No, it's your bottom that makes you look fat.

You get it? You'd certainly get something if you were this honest! I like the story about the husband who has some bad news for his wife. He is at home while she is out enjoying some 'retail therapy'. (He needs therapy when he finds out how much she's spent!)

He calls her on her mobile and declares, 'The cat is dead.'
'What?' she replies.
'He fell off the roof and broke his neck,' he explains.

'That's terrible. You might have broken the news gently to me,' she says.

'What do you mean?' he asks.

'Well, you could have said that your lovely fluffy kitten was chasing a bird and climbed up onto the roof. He was tiptoeing along the gutter when he slipped. He tried to hang on but sadly fell. I tried all I could to revive him but he passed away peacefully in my arms. He would have felt no pain.'

'Oh, I see. I'll remember that in future,' he replies.

Well, the next day his wife is out playing tennis while he is at home mending a curtain rail. The telephone rings and he receives some terrible news that he has to tell his wife. But this time he remembers what she said yesterday and calls her on her mobile.

'Darling, your lovely fluffy mother was chasing a bird and climbed up on to the roof. She was tiptoeing along the gutter when ...'

Honesty is a noble trait and good character matters. Yet sometimes we have to balance the feelings of others along with the need to be straight with people. A Frenchman I once met said English people are too polite. When they disagree they usually say, 'I agree, but ...' A Frenchman will say, 'I don't agree. That's stupid. Now let's have a glass of wine.'

I think I prefer the French way.

There are many rules we're given when we're young and here are a few more you might like to consider:

- Don't touch.

- Speak when you're spoken to.

- Put things back where you found them.

- Look people in the eye.

- Play quietly.

- Don't be shy.

- Take your hands out of your pockets.

If I take all these rules at face value, interpret them literally and don't apply them selectively, I'll become very isolated, withdrawn and unable to integrate in social situations.

So what strategies have I learned? How have I formulated an escape plan? What's been helpful?

I've learned first of all to question the rules. It's okay to ask, 'Why?'

Hmm, some of you are thinking that can be annoying. The child that keeps saying 'Why?' after every parent's reply usually ends up with a final answer of 'Because I said so!' I naturally like to ask questions because I'm inquisitive (not inquisitorial!). So the reasons for rules pose a challenge when I ask people because I'm looking for the outcome and alternatives. I'm also very tempted to break a rule if it seems stupid. A small placard with the text 'Do not walk on the grass' is urging me to walk on the lawn. After all, I can't exactly glide over it and there's no indication of the penalty I could incur if I squash the grass underfoot. That leads me on to my second strategy.

After I've questioned why the rule is there and discovered there's no real danger of serious penalty, I might try to ignore it. What? Ignore the rule? Sure. I'm going to put my hands in my pockets if they're cold. I'm going to touch things if I want to and I'm going to put things back where they ought to be rather than where I found them. I'm not going to let the fear stop me. Being able to take a risk is a huge step for some, but I genuinely believe each step is worth it in the walk of personal freedom.

My last strategy is to talk with a trusted friend about rules. Sometimes if I can't figure it out, my friend will help. We'll discuss and debate topics. We might not agree, but our friendship is not founded on agreement but on love, respect and honesty. In any case, my friend doesn't mind if I disagree, because he's someone who's still learning too. Our friendship has allowed me to live a freer life by helping me see that I can make my own decisions and mistakes and that I don't have to please everyone. He's helped me to recognise the significant things above the trivial.

I think this last strategy is the most effective and life-changing. The influence of others is quite often the thing that breaks a cycle or helps us re-evaluate to change beliefs and direction. Some people might say they don't have many friends. I'd ask, 'Who said the rule was about numbers?'

9

The Ability to Fly

'The role of a clown and a
physician are the same – it's to elevate
the possible and to relieve suffering.'

PATCH ADAMS

Have you noticed how warning labels on products
have become ridiculous? For example, 'May cause
drowsiness' on a bottle of sleeping tablets or 'Remove
child before folding' on a baby stroller. My favourite is
a warning on a Superman cape: 'The wearing of this
cape will not enable you to fly.'

In this book I have extolled the virtues of high-functioning
autism and Asperger's-type conditions based on my
experience and that of others. You may have read everything
and assumed that the wearing of the autism cape will enable
someone to fly. It's true there are huge advantages, and if you

gave me the choice, I would elect to have autism rather than remove it. I don't need curing.

Yet I would not be serving well the many individuals who suffer mental health issues who also have autism. Autism for them has not enabled them to fly. The mental health of the nation is slowly appearing from the gloom as a topic we can face. Mental health is not something to be hidden away and never discussed and so I've decided to devote a chapter to highlight several issues. Boy, is this going to be a tough – but worthwhile – chapter to write.

Confidence

People on the spectrum may appear withdrawn and lack confidence around others. It's the unfamiliar territory that may give this impression, but let me share something with you that might help you and people on the spectrum.

Have you ever met one of those confident types? You know, the one who seems to have it all together and for whom everything in life appears great. Have you ever wondered what their secret is? How did they get there? I bet most of them are pretending. Just a moment … could that be the answer to changing the way I feel? Could pretending actually hold the key?

I grew up shy and introverted and yet today I can address an audience. How come? I pretend. The real 'me' is there, but I observe what confident people look and act like. Shoulders back, head high and good preparation before I open my mouth. The last one has been invaluable in my marriage!

My friend told me about how his children earned their pocket money, which involved pretending. They'd be paid two amounts of money for cutting the grass. One amount was for the cutting and the other amount was what he called 'attitude money'. You see, while they were cutting the grass, they had to pretend that they were enjoying the task. Can you imagine that? Well, years later my friend's children recalled the strategy and the 'attitude money' they could earn. The thing was, they had to admit that by pretending to enjoy the task they actually really did enjoy it. Pretending to have fun changed their attitude and became reality.

When we think we lack confidence, perhaps the thing to do is look at how confident people behave and copy them. If they walk tall, then let's try it. If they shake someone's hand firmly, let's give that one a go. I think people lack confidence in areas they don't understand or have limited knowledge about. When someone says they have no confidence, I'll ask about their interests and hobbies. They usually then have no difficulty sharing their knowledge and expertise. They become very confident people. So, if the issue is knowledge, then the strategy has to be to get knowledge and understanding in all sorts of things.

Self-esteem

How valuable is someone who has autism? It's a strange question to ask, but I've seen children with autism treated less favourably at school than children without a disability. Isn't that disability discrimination? Sometimes. More often than not it's the unconscious belief that everyone should be able to behave in exactly the same way as anyone else. Yet autism may mean a child cannot control their behaviour all the time. They are consistently inconsistent. By the way, did I mention I was always in trouble at school?

Take a child with a physical disability and the response may be different to those who have a neurological or developmental disability. Children and adults are referred to sometimes as having a 'learning disability'. I rather choose to believe that society has a teaching disability; most of us can learn – we just have to be taught in a way we can understand. The truth is sometimes hard to stomach: people with disabilities are not always welcome. The fact that there have to be laws to protect our rights proves that society has not reformed itself.

So what does this do to someone's self-esteem and self-belief? Whenever someone tells me they have Asperger's or are on the spectrum, I usually spend five or ten minutes encouraging them about the positive aspects of their condition. They all know the negatives, but few people have had it explained to them that they may have an advantage or – dare I say – a gift. Usually, the people I speak to want to hear more because they begin to see themselves differently. I'm so grateful to my friend, who has continued to invest encouragement in my life. He's enabled me to see that my life matters and I have something wonderful to contribute to the world. Could you do the same for someone too?

Someone once said, 'Never look down on someone except to lift them up.' That's great advice.

Loneliness

I guess it's not hard to imagine that if someone has difficulty with social situations, feels awkward around others or says the wrong thing at the most inappropriate time, they can become isolated. Not only can they become isolated but they can become the object of ridicule or the butt of a joke. What's worse is that they probably don't understand why this is happening to them and what to do about it. It's something I remember all too well. Even today I have few friends, but I've learned that the game isn't about numbers.

Back in my teenage days, the sense of being alone was, at times, overwhelming. Somehow I didn't fit in and I was teased. Add to that my inability to know who was my friend and if I was liked, and you'll start to see how loneliness and isolation were not too far away. I've observed other children and adults on the spectrum and it's loneliness resulting from isolation that is quite common. I see others speak with them and then walk away to be with more extroverted people. It's understandable – we all have our natural bias and I'm not trying to make people feel guilty. What I'm doing here is pointing out something that is common in society and especially for people with autism conditions. Some of us are lucky and we've learned to love our own company, but others have shrunk away and become sad. For them it's not simple to put into words the incredible loneliness they feel inside because they cannot connect with others when they really need to. From what I've read and seen, girls are less frequently diagnosed because the traits they display are either different from boys or they mask them well. Whereas boys have difficulty hiding behaviour issues and are more frequently referred for diagnosis, girls seem to succeed academically and fly under the radar at school when it comes to behaviour. Their autism may be easily missed and they suffer in silence. Their loneliness and pain can lead to self-harm.

Self-harm

I can't say I've ever deliberately self-harmed, but in today's society it happens a great deal – in secret, behind closed doors and hidden by those who suffer. It includes people cutting themselves, poisoning themselves, over-eating or under-eating, burning their skin, inserting objects into their body, hitting themselves or walls, overdosing, exercising excessively or scratching and hair-pulling. Statistically, girls seem to self-harm more than boys, but I'm not sure we can draw definitive conclusions because so much is hidden from public view. What I do know is that self-harm occurs across all social classes, ages, genders and nationalities. I've asked someone else to explain their experience so we can understand rather than judge. These are their words and I'm grateful they decided to be courageous and share them with us. You'll see they eventually replaced one coping strategy with another, finding something less harmful that still made them feel better.

> Around the age of 14, I self-harmed. For me, it was a way to cope daily and release any negative emotions and feelings that I had. It released a feeling that made me feel better at the time. Eventually, I got to the point

where I felt like I needed to do it continuously and struggled to stop. When I wanted to self-harm, I would be experiencing a 'low'. This could be triggered by things people said to me or events that happened. For example, I once had a teacher in English who did not understand that I struggled in this subject. By the end of a double lesson, focussed on essay practice, I had accomplished no more than writing the essay title. The teacher shouted at me in front of the whole class, displaying my 'appalling' work. I felt really angry and upset by this. At this stage in my life, I was on my road to recovery with self-harm but the first thing I wanted to do was just that. Sometimes, I would get unkind comments or insensitive questions such as 'How many friends do you actually have?' This was said to me many times and every time I felt hurt by it. It would take over my thoughts, which triggered lows leading to self-harm.

Parents often blame themselves for their child's self-harm. However, no matter how much a parent blames themselves, it really is not their fault. In fact, I don't see it as any individual's fault. People may have said or done something that contributed to my feelings on their bad day or without realising it, but the self-harm is not the parent's fault. It is a coping strategy. A way to feel even the slightest bit 'normal' or 'better'.

In the time that I did self-harm, if I had been stopped by someone or I couldn't access what I needed to self-harm, I would become agitated and anxious. I would feel the need to lash out or physically release my emotions through hitting something, usually a table or wall. I never wanted to hurt anyone through my self-harm because, actually, it felt like my fault that I felt that way. Not being able to self-harm when I needed to could trigger emotional meltdowns or panic attacks.

During my recovery there were three key things that helped me and I'd like to share them with you:

1. Provide a mentor. I needed to know there was someone I could go to who was open to listen when I needed to vent or even to just cry. Someone who wouldn't judge me or simply tell me to just 'pull myself together'.

2. Encouragement rather than discouragement. I needed a lot of reminding of the good things I had achieved. Not necessarily the big things or academic things – the small things are important too. I eventually recorded all the little good things each day in a book. This really helped me.

3. Allow time and space to process events and to calm down by myself. This is important as it can be very overwhelming being around people all the time. A place, particularly in school, where I could withdraw from everyone was helpful.

Depression

When I was 15, I remember feeling low almost every day for approximately six months. It was agony and arrived at my doorstep because of my loneliness. It was a progression from isolation, and it was a struggle to see any light or happiness at the end of the dark tunnel. My feelings of worthlessness led me to a place of not wanting to live. I had thoughts of suicide but never went that far – something deep inside pulled me back from the edge. It was like being lost without knowing what I needed to help me find my way home. It was a valley of deep darkness.

I'm no expert and I don't have all the answers, but I'm aware the journey to a brighter place is possible with the support of others. The external influence of someone's love becomes the warmth in the cold place that can bring us back. What we need isn't always obvious to us but it usually involves someone else. My friend helps people escape these places, and one thing he teaches is all about posture. The way we stand can affect the way we feel. Counting chimneys may seem strange, but the strategy isn't about counting – it's about raising our heads, looking up and changing our posture. I've understood from others that depression is an illness that needs treatment, and if that's the case, then I have to believe there is a cure and I have to believe it comes with the support of others.

Suicide

The largest cause of death among 19- to 40-year-old men in England and Wales isn't cancer. Neither is it heart disease or car accidents. Suicide is the biggest killer and it's a shocking statistic. Women may talk about feelings of suicide, but men just do it. Others self-harm without intending to end their lives but do so accidentally by overdose. Those left behind will always wonder what they could have done. Why didn't they see any signs? There's no closure and they feel guilty.

Autism doesn't strip away confidence or cause low self-esteem, it doesn't make a person lonely or depressed and it doesn't make a person suicidal. The cause of these things are, in my view, linked to how people are treated, the circumstances they find themselves in and their inner thoughts. But autism may make a person more susceptible to these issues because they see the world differently, lack an ability to easily connect with others and need to withdraw to de-stress from the world they are so sensitive to.

If you have suicidal thoughts, you are not alone. Famous people, ordinary people, rich people and poor people go through this agony. Please step back from the edge and choose to live. Don't let the moment decide your life must end – ask for help. Those you would leave need you – your life matters. There is a better way out of feeling so unwell.

A better way out

Throughout this book I've sought to encourage and present an angle on autism that's a little different. I've promoted the positive idea that my autism is a gift without which I'd achieve less than I have and perhaps the lives of those around me would be a little less enriched. My 'insider' understanding brings a perspective that perhaps those in the medical profession can only read about second-hand. It's this unusual position that I find myself in that has helped me find a place of usefulness. I'm glad my life has continued and that I never ended it in my teenage years. Looking back, I could never have imagined where I'd be in the future, but I'm pleased to have found fulfilment in serving others with my life. I've learned to believe that my life is a gift to the world, which has helped me to have a better view of myself, my value and how I'm not meant to fit in. In fact, not fitting in has enabled me to do so much more.

My life seems really busy at the moment and people ask where I find the time to do everything. Truth is, keeping busy with worthwhile things helps me focus on the positive. I know there are negative thoughts and darkness lurking behind me. Sometimes I catch them in the corner of my eye, but that's as far as I will allow them to come. Most of the time they're kept far behind me. Even on 'bad' days I know that a good night's sleep will help and that the next morning can bring happiness because I choose to believe it will be a brighter day.

The pursuit of happiness is part of the American Declaration of Independence drafted by Thomas Jefferson. He understood its importance to every individual and enshrined it as a right given by the Creator to all human beings. Interestingly, there is speculation that Thomas Jefferson, the third US President, may have been autistic. It's recorded that he was shy, had an inability to relate to others, had difficulties in public speaking and was sensitive to loud noises. He wasn't great at managing his finances, and although he kept an accurate record of all of his spending, he died in debt. He obsessively remodelled his home and was very eccentric. Jefferson had some unusual behaviours and it's said that he even wore slippers to important meetings. He collected books and even after selling some he admitted he couldn't live without them and purchased more. Yet this man contributed to society. He could speak French, Greek, Italian, Latin and Spanish. He was self-taught by reading and became a lawyer. He was a great architect and inventor. He had numerous inventions that he gave freely to posterity and his idea of interchangeable parts led to modern industry. He improved the design of the pedometer and the printing press and even invented the first swivel chair. Before he died he said, 'I have done for my country, and for all mankind, all that I could do.' He did so much, even though he battled with depression which was the result of tough circumstances.

Recognising what we're naturally good at and working towards it has to be one of the ways that helps us to focus towards something great rather than restrict our view to the things people say we're lacking. I've said it before: pursuing what we're good at makes perfect sense and discovering new aspects to an underlying talent brings variety. Believe there's more to come.

You've probably guessed I have a sense of humour and look out for opportunities for fun. I cultivated these two things even in the darkest times and they've brought me relief and release. Many say people with autism spectrum conditions are immature by, say, five years or so. So a 14-year-old may only cope with the responsibility an 11-year-old can handle. It's not necessarily a lack of intelligence – in fact, many people with Asperger's syndrome are above average in that department. Now, if you're a little immature (like me), I'd say, 'Take advantage of it.' It doesn't have to be completely negative, because there's something lovely about the innocence or naivety of some people. The ability to not take things too seriously and seek out fun lightens life for us and everyone around us. Only the other week I was on a train with my wife when the ticket inspector walked through the carriage asking to see tickets. I held out my ticket and said, 'Here's mine. My wife hasn't got one so could you throw her off?' The conductor laughed while my wife elbowed me in the ribs.

The last point I'd like to make is that we need others to help us. Life is tough, and people with autism can be easily discouraged by others. Equally, we can be encouraged to press on up the hill. When you take time to come alongside someone who's struggling and encourage them, it makes all the difference. Reminding them of how they have helped you or others, what a difference they make and how they are needed make great conversation subjects. Don't give up on them – they need you to stick with them because it may take them longer to let you in. Remember, a long-term problem may require a long-term solution.

Children and young people with autism are sensitive souls: they become anxious, they become distressed, they become afraid. If I label everything as an emotional meltdown, I have no clue what to do about their rush of unbearable feelings. But if someone is anxious, distressed or afraid, I can reassure them, I can support them, I can protect them. Calling something what it is enables me to see the solution, and I've found this approach far more helpful than just using the term 'meltdown'.

If you're the one struggling, you've got to make a decision: either to struggle alone or to let someone help you. The former is possible, but there's no shame in asking for support when you need it. That takes courage and a courageous person like you only needs to say, 'Help me.'

Not long ago I was at a training day for potential associate hospital managers for a local health authority. I'd gone there to see if it was something I could help with, but in the end I decided the NHS didn't really need my help. I've learned not to say 'yes' to everything because a 'yes' to one thing is a 'no' to something else. Anyway, at lunchtime I went for a walk and saw an elderly lady dressed in an expensive-looking coat, makeup meticulously applied and not a hair out of place. She could have been royalty the way she looked. I quite like watching people and I've become more observant as I've become older. I watched her shuffle along with a walking aid and, looking more intently, I saw that her back was curved, which caused her to look down at the path rather than ahead. She then approached a road where she began to struggle with her walking frame. It had wheels at the front but she couldn't step on to the road from the kerb. I jogged over and asked if she needed some help, which she affirmed with the words, 'I can't get the wheels down on to the road.' I gently lifted the wheels off the kerb and the lady carried on walking across the road with her head still down. While she crossed, I stopped the traffic as she seemed unaware of the danger. Once on the other side, she continued down the pavement towards the town shops. I'd helped her with just what she needed and then let her be independent again.

It occurs to me that even though she was impeccably dressed and had the appearance of royalty, first impressions don't give the whole picture. Only as I observed did it become apparent that she needed help. The strange thing was that everyone else ignored her. I was the only one who seemed to notice she was having difficulty. It was almost as if what she was wearing hid her problem. That's something we might like to learn from: outward appearances may hide the struggle we feel inside. We sometimes need to ask for help as well as become more sensitive and observant to the needs of others. Help is there not to make us dependent but to meet an immediate need so we can continue along the path and be independent again. There's no shame in asking for help.

I'll be honest with you. This has been a difficult chapter to write. At times I've wondered if I should include it, but I've dared to take the risk because I genuinely care and want to help as many people as I can. I have personally faced most of the difficulties above and I've not pretended the autism cape will enable everyone to fly. However, I've challenged us to believe that there is something truly great within us that brings meaning and purpose in our lives – whether we have an autism condition or not. Life is worth living and we can choose to believe in possibilities not impossibilities.

10

Getting Through the Tough Stuff of Change

'Sometimes if you want to see a change for the better, you have to take things into your own hands.'

CLINT EASTWOOD

Two identical-looking caterpillars were sitting on a leaf when they observed a beautiful butterfly glide past. They both looked at each other and one said to the other, 'There's no way you're going to get me up in one of those things!'

I wanted to include this chapter because I addressed a group of parents facing the challenge of transition. Change was happening right in front of them and they needed some encouragement as their children began the difficult road from childhood to adulthood. I took the group through some of the things I'd found helpful and, judging by the responses, there was something useful there for everyone.

Some of the things you'll recognise from other chapters, but they're worth reinforcing when we're helping our teenagers move into adulthood. We have no choice – just as caterpillars change into something else, our children will grow up and change too. So let me encourage you.

It's tough being a parent

I've not met anyone who would disagree with this statement and yet many feel guilty that they don't do enough. I've mentioned before that it's not your fault if your child has autism, so please don't take the guilt trip. You know, we do the best we can with what we have when it comes to parenting and I think it's our most important role. You see, we might take a job, but we *become* a parent. There's no guidebook or instruction manual that comes with a newborn and yet somehow we manage to adapt.

Being a parent is about letting go. We have to prepare our son or daughter to become an adult, and that takes time and an investment of good things into their life. It means setting boundaries and it means removing them too. Why? Because we want our children to live and enjoy the best life they can. Your child is worth the investment of love.

My experience as a parent has had its ups and downs, just like any other. Our problems may be different, but we all have struggles. My wife and I faced school exclusions, issues around drugs, a child who suffered depression and self-harmed, and another who at times felt suicidal. We've cried and laughed together, held each other through the dark days and kept going even when we felt like giving up. We've been in situations where, quite frankly, we couldn't see what the end might be. But my wife and I never stopped loving even if we didn't understand. We've faced physical violence, verbal abuse and blatant defiance. We've seen a child leave us and then years later return and tell us that they love us.

There is one story I remember I want to share. I was waiting in a police station late at night because one of my children had been arrested. I didn't know if they would be charged but I do remember just waiting, powerless to do anything to rewind the clock. Opposite me sat a girl who must have been about 20. She was slim, had dark hair and looked as if she'd been in trouble. She looked across at me and explained that she'd been arrested for drugs and was waiting to be released. She told me she had a young child who was being brought up by her mother. Her life was a mess and I think she had fallen out with her family.

What do you say to someone like that? Lacking social etiquette, I seem to be able to talk to strangers. So I explained why I was there and ended by saying something I'd never said before: 'You know, your mum still loves you. You never stop loving your children.' Her eyes welled up.

It's true, isn't it? You never stop loving. You never stop caring. And where there's love, then there's hope.

Change is going to happen so don't fight to maintain the status quo

Can you imagine a world without change? Would that be a good thing? Would we enjoy that? I guess we'd like some things to never change, but that would be based on our experience. If things never changed, then we'd miss out on new experiences we might enjoy or new friends we've yet to meet. Some people tell me they'd like to go back to their youth, but I remind them that back then there was algebra.

So, if we accept change is going to happen, perhaps we can be a little more prepared in our mind and attitude? Trying to keep things just as they are and preserving the status quo probably won't do anyone any favours. I want my children to experience the world and live, and I just love the following advice:

> Life should NOT be a journey to the grave with the intention of arriving safely in an attractive and well-preserved body, but rather to skid in sideways, chocolate in one hand, martini in the other, body thoroughly used up, totally worn out and screaming, 'WOO-HOO, what a ride!'

Choose your battles

Deciding what's important and what's not significant is, in my view, important when deciding the boundaries you put in place. Regardless of who comes into your home or their age, remember your home is yours. That means you decide the rules and you decide what's important and why. Although compromise is important in negotiating responsibilities, it doesn't replace the understanding of what's right or wrong and that your home is a place of safety for everyone. My home is a place free from drugs and violence. That's a point on which I won't negotiate. Our children are welcome to live with us, provided they don't bring in drugs or are violent, because our home is a haven for everyone.

As your child enters teenage years and then approaches adulthood, you still need boundaries in your home, but the life decisions need to be passed over to them. You shouldn't decide their career or interests – they have to do that for themselves. Your child has to live their life, and part of a parent's job is to facilitate that, guide them and let them set sail by themselves. You give them as much responsibility as they can handle. Some can handle more than others, so you can't treat every child the same. But you can treat every child fairly.

Let me illustrate responsibility with a simple example. Many parents may take the view that because a child has a disability they must do everything for them. That, in my view, harbours the belief that their child is incapable of learning, which I don't accept. I have, wherever possible, enabled my children to make their own choices. Whenever we could afford to eat out at a restaurant, if our son or daughter was old enough to talk we had a rule that said they had to order their own food. We might help them a little, but the transition was all about understanding that the waiter/waitress was there to help and that they were allowed to ask for what they wanted. They had to make the choice and they had to learn not to be afraid or they wouldn't eat. They also had to be polite – we never tolerated rudeness and we always said they should never look down on people who served them and they should always be grateful. Today, all my children can go out with friends and order their own food. They aren't shy of restaurant staff and I can trust them to be polite and thankful. Start them young. You see, they were given freedom alongside important boundaries to guide and teach them life skills.

Let's talk

There are many parents and children who don't communicate. It's really sad, but I want to say that it doesn't have to stay like that and you can choose to finish well. Sometimes children leave and come back and the relationship changes for the better. Other times people are not so lucky. So address this issue early rather than struggle with things later.

If I was to use one word to describe the cause of communication failure, it would be this: erosion. Over a period of days, weeks, months and years the communication dwindles and silence or shouting replaces conversation. How and when did this start? What event led to it? Because if we could reverse time, we'd agree that, whatever it was, it wasn't worth losing the ability to communicate. It's time to buy back the years and start to talk again. Do something kind that provokes a response. Keep being kind. Persevere and keep telling the other person you love them.

When we really engage with one another, we become interested in what the other is saying. Their point of view is valid. We listen to understand rather than to answer back.

Less hasty to judge, we begin to help by sharing other points of view rather than dictate our standpoint. We might not agree but we'll never find out if we don't share.

I often found that when talking with someone with autism it's easier not to press home a strong point of view about something that's not that important. We might do things differently and actually be right, but the way we express our opinion can't be easily accepted by the listener. A suggestion of ideas to explore removes the sense that we're the authority. Do you remember that people with autism struggle with authority? So allowing them to work through choices can be less stressful for everyone. Teenagers need this as well as boundaries. Young children definitely need boundaries, and parents should retain responsibility. So how do I offer younger ones choice? Let me give you an example that focusses on the outcome rather than the request.

It's easy to say, 'You must go to bed now.' But that can come across as confrontational and is less easy to obey than a choice. Choice would say, 'Would you like me to carry you to bed or would you like to walk?' You're giving choice but the outcome is the same: it's bed time. Offering alternatives that have the same result when a child is young can be adjusted for when a child is in their teens. Consider the following statements:

- Are you working on your homework today or at the weekend?

- I really need someone to help me with this.

- How do I do this better? Can you show me?

- Have you thought about this option?

- I know you're clever enough to understand that there are other points of view. What do you think they might be?

It takes practice. Sometimes I jokingly say to my daughter, 'Of course you can choose. It's your life and you can mess it up any way you like.' She usually smiles and sarcastically says, 'Ha ha.' Choice is king and that's probably why I like Neapolitan ice cream.

Have you noticed sometimes (maybe always?) that when someone who has autism talks they let everything out really quickly? A torrent of ideas, thoughts and subjects just spill out everywhere and you're wondering what to do?

People with autism quite often have busy minds. Together with the processing of their environment, they can be easily distracted and jump from one subject to another. What they need is time, so it's helpful to sit down with them and tell them that they have your undivided attention until they have finished. Tell them there is no rush. Help them to slow their speech down and this will reduce their stress. I often struggled with communication at school because teachers didn't give me time to process requests or say what I needed to say. I stumbled over my words. Today I've learned to slow down. I still lose words because my mind is distracted; in the middle of a sentence I may know what to say, but the word I need is missing. Or I have a new thought and idea but lose it while in conversation. I desperately try to remember and bring it back, and I end up scrambling through the forest of my mind until I find it. To help with this I sometimes carry a notebook and write a thought down – it saves getting lost in the forest. Similarly, interrupting me causes me to lose my place and sometimes I have to go back to the beginning.

You see, my mind is so busy that ideas and thoughts pop in and out all the time. It never seems to rest until I sleep – even then I can wake up with an idea. Every thought is like a butterfly, flitting around me. I try to catch it and then another one appears. And then another and then another. I'm catching butterflies all day. The thing is that once I've caught one, I don't get to enjoy it because I keep trying to catch the others.

What I've learned to do is catch a few butterflies and leave the others. I'm tempted to carry on catching but that distracts me. So I watch them come and go. If I notice a particularly beautiful one, I'll catch it and write down my thought. You might be wondering if this is stressful. Sometimes it's frustrating, but I don't want my mind to change. The ability to have all these 'butterflies' provides me with solutions to problems or an inventiveness and creativity I enjoy. It's part of me. It's particularly useful when I read social law, because when reading one piece of legislation, another piece appears and I can join two ideas together. I read complex things and seem to understand them. I don't know how – I just do.

Now you understand how busy my mind is and how it works, perhaps that will clarify why time and space to talk is important. Give it a go.

The social world

I've already devoted Chapter 6 to social situations, but let's reiterate and add a few useful points.

Going out for a meal is all about the company and not what's on the menu. Teenagers with autism need to be shown and taught this so they can join in. The laughter, conversation and 'messing about' is all part and parcel of the experience. What's not appropriate at home for young children changes when teens and adults enjoy a meal together. We've got to loosen up and let go a little. And that leads on to my next point about unlearning rules.

In Chapter 8 I explained the importance of helping young people to unlearn rules in readiness for adulthood. What was useful as a child proves a hindrance when blending into the social group. Show by example that certain rules don't apply and explain why. Quite often young children with autism are looking for permission to do things differently.

Friendship is all about quality and not quantity. That's the new rule to introduce to a young person. How many friends do you need at one time? The social media site that encourages us to add new friends isn't a replacement for personal social connection. People are an essential ingredient in life, and enabling your teen to be in places where he or she can discover new friends is going to help them. The era of being the parent taxi company may be inconvenient, but I think it's another way of demonstrating our love and commitment to our children.

Lastly, home is a place of safety for young people. Or it should be. Creating an environment where your child feels safe (that means boundaries for everyone), loved and accepted by what you say and do means they'll have somewhere to come if things don't work out. I have to admit that I'm relaxed at home – it's as good as a holiday. I know we all like to get away, but I love my home because there I find the most important people in my life and a place of love, laughter and acceptance. Oh, that's another useful tip: add plenty of laughter and fun.

Taking on responsibility and making decisions and choices

The ability to make decisions and choices was something I found hard as a teenager. I'm now in my 40s and I think I'm getting there! The issue that makes me hesitant is knowing whether I have permission or authority to make those choices. At work it's clearly defined, although I choose to make myself accountable. However, new situations and environments make me a little nervous. So a clear lead and direction from someone else is required to help me understand that the decision is up to me.

When we help our children make the transition from childhood to adulthood, we're giving them permission to make life decisions for themselves. We're letting go of the reins and reassuringly watching nearby to see what happens and if they can cope with the responsibility. I mentioned before that many people with autism lag behind when it comes to maturity, but that only means they need some time to catch up. Be patient and be available. Give them as much responsibility as they can handle. 'Less controlling and more supportive' is a good approach. Let them make unimportant mistakes so they can learn that life has its ups and downs and that there's a strategy to learn when it goes wrong. The strategy usually involves asking for help and being shown rather than told what to do. Start your child young so that the transition is less painful for you both later on.

One last point here. As far as possible, never interfere with an employer/employee relationship unless it's absolutely essential. As an employer, I know it can create bad feeling and may undermine a child's prospects if they are seen not to be able to speak for themselves. My daughter once asked me to help and I placed a limit on what I'd do. I told her what was right and then left her to approach her employer politely. She managed to sort out the issue and gained confidence and important experience. Mum and Dad won't always be there.

Changing the way we think and making room for grey areas

Life has a funny way of surprising us. Just when we thought we had it all worked out and put everything neatly into various compartments, something else sneaks in that doesn't fit. Life's not a department store with everything laid out perfectly. You'll know that if you're a parent: along comes this little person with no instruction manual. It's interesting that of all the health visitors I've met, none have had children. Instead, they had dogs or cats. Did learning *about* children put them off *having* children? The difference between a health visitor and a parent is like eggs and bacon – a day's work for the chicken but a lifelong commitment for the pig. (I'm not saying parents are pigs – don't take the analogy too far!)

People with autism may prefer routine and order, and some behave like clockwork: the same daily home routine, the same route to work or the same activity when they get to work. So how do you change the cycle and introduce randomness? It's not easy and I'd be the first to check out why I want to introduce the change. Is it really that important?

I think learning to adapt to a changing world is a useful tool. One way I've encouraged 'routine huggers' is to pick the same time each day and do something random or different. Do you get that? There's order – 'the same time' – and there's variety – 'something random'. Little steps are best. It challenges thinking and that opens up possibilities.

Popping random ideas into a conversation allows the possibility of considering options. Giving the other person permission to think differently about something offers them the freedom to decide for themselves. For example, my friend would probably explore possibilities and ask open questions that help people to be less dismissive of their abilities. Instead of believing we can't do something, my friend would probably ask us, 'What do you need so you can make that happen?' Do you remember the maze in Chapter 3? It's all about working backwards.

They say example is the best way to lead. But it's not – it's the *only* way. How you live your life will affect your children. The freedom and randomness of your life will demonstrate to them that life can be wobbly and that's okay. If we create fixed and predictable environments for our children, then they just might struggle more in a topsy-turvy world.

Learning to enjoy life
because it's not all bad!

I'm on a crusade. It's called 'Enjoy the wobble!'

It's never too late to start. Whatever has gone before needn't hold us back. That was then – this is now. There may be tough times, but remember there will be great times too.

It seems the world has a different campaign. The stories we read and the news we watch are predominantly focussed on the negative. Even the weather forecast talks about a 10 per cent chance of rain rather than a 90 per cent chance of sunshine. If you live in Africa, 10 per cent could spark hope in a drought.

When we hear of terrible crimes, mass killings by an individual who goes on some kind of rampage or someone incarcerated in an institution for a psychopathic crime, the press seems to drop in an irrelevant fact such as 'They have Asperger's'. It creates a negative association. The world thinks anyone with an autism-type condition is a danger to society and capable of an awful act against mankind. It's as if the condition causes the crime. Is it any wonder parents begin to worry?

I want to flip the coin and say that without autism the world would be worse off. Those with autism can contribute to society in amazing ways. Their intelligence, perseverance and single-mindedness have caused breakthroughs and progress down the ages. It's not all bad. In fact, I don't believe autism directly causes crime. I think it has more to do with how people treat each other and other mental health issues.

It's easy to understand why life can feel incredibly lonely for a parent with a child who has autism. It's also possible to understand the loneliness of those who have autism. I fit both categories: I'm a parent with children on the autistic spectrum and I also have autism. The difference is I've made the decision to accept the condition as a gift and advantage. I've sought out the positives and focussed on the great. Sure, I struggle at social gatherings. Sure, I get lonely. Sure, I don't fit in. But I'm amazed at what I've achieved because of autism. I really don't suffer from autism – I excel because of it.

Learning to value and enjoy the uncertainty of life and the wobbles it brings has to do with knowing that tough times produce character and perseverance. I like to think that we learn more through difficulties and solving problems than we do when everything in the garden is lovely. I'm not advocating pretending tough days are easy. Let's be honest: tough means tough. There will be tears, sadness, anger and frustration. I'd never play down someone's tragedy – they need a friend not a critic. It's not for me to dictate how they should feel. But I intend to get the best out of the situation and to milk it for the positive things I can learn and extract. Why? Because I can use the experience to help others along and understand better what really is tough and what's not.

If I chose to view my life as a long marathon of misery and endurance, my sighs would become longer, my complaints louder and more frequent, and my frowns would become broader. I'd stop enjoying life, and those around me would drift away into the shadows. Guess what? I'm not going there. I've made a choice to laugh, have fun and fool around a little. I'm looking for the sparkle, and if it's not there, I want to bring it. Will you join me? It's never too late to start. Having an attitude that's grateful for what we have and what we can do helps enormously to propel us onwards and upwards.

Are you ready to enjoy the wobble?

11

Love, Sweet Love

'Any man who can
drive a car safely while kissing
a pretty girl is simply not giving
the kiss the attention it deserves.'

*ATTRIBUTED TO
ALBERT EINSTEIN*

There's a story about a man called Bob who fell head over heels in love with a woman called Jean. Despite Bob dropping her hints, buying her flowers and chocolates, Jean just didn't seem interested. She wasn't really in love with Bob but was never unkind to him – she didn't want to hurt his feelings. But her kindness just made things worse because Bob could only conclude she was even more wonderful. After several months of trying to gain her affections, Bob had to move abroad on business. Bob was not deterred from trying to win Jean over and wrote to her almost every day. Bob thought to himself, 'If I write all these letters, she's bound to know I love her.'

Bob sent more than 700 letters and eventually Jean fell in love…and married the postman.

If you read the text books on autism, you'd be forgiven for thinking that autistic people never fall in love and certainly never get married. The rule seems to be that they just don't make the connection and love passes them by. I guess I broke that rule.

Listen, let me tell you something. Just because someone has an autistic mind it doesn't mean they don't have feelings or fall in love. They might find it difficult to express those emotions but they're just as real as anyone else's. Some people ask, 'Do they want intimacy and closeness?' Yes! Our brains may be wired a little differently, but everything else is intact!

I've been married for 25 years to the same person and I've never loved another the way I love her. Sure I'm old-fashioned but I like the idea of marriage. The commitment to work through stuff and stay together has to be the best formula I know. Sometimes the ideal doesn't always work out and I'm not judging you if you're divorced or living together. However, now that I've dispelled the myth about falling in love and intimacy, I want to share things I've learned about a relationship when one person has autism. It's kind of a question-and-answer session and I've based it on what I've been asked before.

Do you think love is enough?

I like the joke about Adam and Eve when Eve says to Adam one day, 'Do you love me?' Adam replies, 'Well, who else is there?'

I think liking someone is a great start, and spending time to gently get to know each other can be very exciting. Telling them you like being together is quite important for someone with autism because they find it difficult to know if they are liked, loved or otherwise. It needs to be said and they need reminding. They need reassurance because, quite often, they have low self-esteem. They don't see themselves as the other person does and you can't take things for granted when it comes to unspoken affection. I probably don't tell my wife enough that I love her. She'd probably say, 'You're too right you don't!' I concede defeat. I know I need to say it more often.

If your partner has autism, I'd say it's worth remembering that they may express their love by what they do. Please don't be discouraged if they aren't too expressive. Likewise, if you have autism, you'd do well to express your love in words, either in little notes or face to face. The one you love needs it to blossom.

I think I express my love by how I help out and by encouraging my wife to go out more often. You're thinking we must argue a lot for me to want her to go out! Not quite. I just want her to be free to pursue her interests because I know our interests may be different. Having different hobbies or interests doesn't mean people cannot stay in love. The important thing is to accept the differences and be an encouragement to one another. There will be times when we share the same activity and times when we'll be apart. That doesn't mean we have nothing in common. What we have in common is love, experiences, our children and the life we've built together.

I could be very possessive but I decided long ago not to be that way. I don't own my wife and I'd rather we were together out of choice than because I controlled her every move. I have many faults and insecurities, but jealousy is not one of them. So in answer to the question 'Do I think love is enough?' I'd say there needs to be a commitment to one another and an understanding to encourage each other to discover new interests and talents. Maybe those are characteristics of love?

How did you meet your wife?

In answer to this question I quite often say, 'We met in a travel agent shop. She was looking for a holiday and I was her last resort.'

The truth is we originally met at the church we both attended and she also worked at the local chip shop. She was 16 and I was 19, and I loved the way she smiled. Sometimes I'd walk her home, but it took me a very long time to work out how to ask her out on a date. Fortunately, she was patient and after cooking her a meal I asked her. What started as friendship blossomed into love, and the rest, as they say, is history (not like the Battle of Britain!).

My advice to you if you have autism is to take things gently. Don't be possessive. Make sure you clean your teeth and shower every day. Use a lovely shower gel and antiperspirant under your arms; others will notice if you don't and might avoid the smell *you* have grown accustomed to. I'm sorry for being so blunt, but someone has to tell you that if you don't take care of your personal hygiene every day, you will stink and the flowers will wilt as you pass them in the park. It's not kind to the wildlife and it's certainly not fair to other people.

If you're the other person in the friendship, you might like to lead a little more, but don't be bossy or commanding because autistic people quite often resist authority either by confrontation or, more often, by withdrawing. Start as friends and see where it leads. Be clear about boundaries because people with autism need clarity. To be blunt again, love isn't just about having sex.

Are you selfish?

Absolutely. Sometimes I'm as stubborn as they get and it's best not to argue with me. If I don't want to do something, there's usually a reason based on past experience or because I'm tired and want time alone. I know I spend time by myself resetting my busy mind. I get grumpy. I get angry. I turn inwards and withdraw. That is selfish.

Yet I'm also capable of selfless acts of kindness to others. I'd like to think that my strengths outweigh the selfishness that doesn't help in a relationship. By the way, not all selfishness is necessarily bad. It is important to have some 'me time' to bring balance to our lives. People with autism need time alone to calm down or clear their heads. If you're not getting anywhere in a conversation with your friend who has autism, give them some space and approach the subject later. You'll probably find they will change their mind or be more engaged once they've had some time alone.

Is there the perfect partner?

What? No, of course not. But you can become very special to someone. Life has a way of changing us over the years and adjustment is necessary all the time. Being a couple means we grow together rather than grow apart. We build a life together and support and encourage each other. Maybe we become the perfect partners for each other rather than start off that way. We learn how to deal with our disagreements and understand each other better the longer we are together. Sometimes I explain to men: 'You see, you spent years looking for Miss Right. You wanted the perfect companion and lover and so searched the country for her. You persevered and never gave up hope that one day you'd meet Miss Right. And when you finally found Miss Right, you proposed and got married. It was only then that you discovered that her first name was Always.'

How do you resolve arguments?

The comedian Les Dawson once said that he and his wife had a wonderful way of resolving their differences. It was called 'boxing'. Two rounds in the ring usually saw her victorious.

Usually, differences occur because we're tired or something's happened to upset us. Having a strong will doesn't help either. After we 'discuss' the issue, sometimes loudly, one of us usually softens to the other, which then leads the other to let go. Sometimes we both shed tears. We're not going to agree all the time but there is a commitment to love each other.

Someone once said that three words have helped to preserve their marriage: 'I'm going out.' Sometimes it is a good idea to find a place to cool down. The following sentences should also be practised:

- I was wrong.

- I am sorry.

- Please forgive me.

- I love you.

How do you know what each other is feeling?

How does anyone know that? It's a deep mystery! Seriously, though, it's important that the other person speaks their mind. We have this openness at home where we say what we think. We can be a bit blunt, but it works for us. The problems occurred when the children were at school and spoke 'bluntly' to teachers. They would come across as rude and several times I had to explain to the teacher that my children say things as they are and no offence is intended. Since my wife isn't on the autistic spectrum, she, I think, has the toughest job.

So how does your wife cope?

She's not yet booked to see a psychiatrist, so I guess she accepts me as I am, just as I accept her. She knows I care and sometimes I like to surprise her by taking her out for a meal to show my appreciation. She'll usually ask if the restaurant has a special offer on or something! That might be true sometimes, but it's the desire to make her feel special that is appreciated.

At times it must be hard for her but, as I've mentioned, I am very happy for her to develop other interests and go out so she can have a break. She tells me she loves me and I couldn't do what I do without her support. We do laugh quite a lot because I see the funny side of things and she gets the one-liners I throw out. Living with me must at times be infuriating when I'm stubborn. Despite this, I have qualities that she probably likes – loyalty, responsibility, reassurance and encouragement.

Have you ever been chatted up by other women?

I probably wouldn't know if I had, because I think people are just being nice. I don't get the whole thing about flirting. However, I do find that the 80-year-old women in my wife's sweet shop can be quite frisky and very naughty. I tell them it's safe to have sex at 70 if they pull over on to the hard shoulder. Boy, it's tough being a sex symbol for women who don't care!

How do you approach the subject of sex with your teenage children?

I take the bull by the horns and I say, 'I'm too young to be a grandfather.' I'm not naive enough to believe the opportunity won't be there, and I'm clear about the need to ensure sex is safe to protect themselves from illness and pregnancy.

Being blunt may seem unorthodox, but people with autism need clarity. I'm not going to discuss the Kama Sutra with them, but I will tell them there are consequences to their actions and what they might be. It's a 'matter of fact' kind of conversation rather than a taboo subject. Parents need to educate their children; if we don't, they'll be educated by their peers or what they watch on television or read in magazines. Is that what we want?

Do you think everyone should have a partner?

Someone once asked me a similar question: 'Do you want your children to get married?' I replied, 'Of course. I suffered, why shouldn't they?'

Whether someone has a partner depends on them. Parents are great at wanting what's best for their children and forget that they might not always be right. Being a couple isn't for everyone, but I do think friendship is important. Whether someone wants to be alone or find someone special will be linked to their own desire to socialise. I know people who are very happy living alone because it allows them to pursue their own interests and come and go as they please, and I understand the need for time to be alone. For me, though, being married makes my life complete, and I always wanted a family. I think if I was widowed, I'd stay single because I'm not sure I would find another like my wife. I've had the best life could offer and I don't think I could top that. I'd devote my time to helping my children and others.

What helps you the most?

That's easy. My wife's smile. Sometimes I cannot tell if I've done something wrong or if I've annoyed her. (All male readers are now frantically agreeing!) I don't pick up facial expressions very well, but I'm told a smile is understood all over the world. When my wife smiles, I know everything is okay. Her smile brings relief when I'm worried or upset. Her smile tells me she loves me.

It was her smile that first attracted me to her.

12

The World Needs Autism

'Sometimes we stare so long
at a door that is closing that we
see too late the one that is open.'

ALEXANDER BELL

A father was praising his young son and encouraging him to grow up into the man he could be proud of. At the end of the conversation the father looked at his son and said, 'And remember above all things that you're unique – just like everyone else.'

The transition from childhood to adulthood is difficult enough, but when someone has autism they approach adulthood with conflicting signals. Their transition becomes a struggle because on the one hand they've been taught to conform and on the other they have a new ideal to become an individual. Conforming and becoming something different – what a challenge!

Have you ever had anyone tell you, 'You're special'? I emailed it to someone once and they emailed me back and said they weren't sure how to take my comment. Was I being complimentary or was I implying something else? What did I mean by 'special'? Was I saying he was different? In reply I suggested to my colleague that he might like to choose from the following list:

- special agent

- special delivery

- special team

- special branch

- special edition

- special forces

- special needs

- special effect

- special offer.

When I visited my grandmother, she made me feel special and I always loved that. So what makes us want to fit in, to be the same or be like someone else, to follow the crowd? People pay real money to see something different. We long for new inventions, new ideas, new trends in fashion and new ways of doing things. And yet we have an aversion to being different. It seems the grass is always greener for others, so we think we ought to aspire to be like them. Not only that, but we actively encourage others to fit the same shape. But stop! Have you never heard the saying 'Never teach a pig to sing'? The people won't like it and it will annoy the pig. In other words, don't try to make others into something they're not.

I listened to an interview in which the singer Lionel Richie explained what he would say to those in the music industry trying to get to the top. I loved his advice. He said about being at the top, 'There's nothing there.' Do you get that? Someone as successful as Lionel Richie says something like that. Wow! It makes you put things in perspective. It tells me to stop trying to climb the corporate ladder just because everyone else is. It tells me that I ought to be cautious about pursuing a course to try to achieve or be the same as everyone else. Their goals are not going to be mine. By not being in step, I approach things from an entirely different angle. I've something unique to contribute just by being myself. I've found the following advice has been an encouragement:

- Know yourself.

- Accept yourself.

- Be the best that you can be.

Not long ago I read an article about 'positive thinking'. It asserted that so much was possible if only we changed the way we think. Although I understand what the writer was trying to convey, I have to admit that the 'positive thinking' we hear so much about doesn't sit comfortably with me when people assert that anything is achievable if we just believe it. Quite often it's used to quell dissention in the ranks and quiet any sort of critical thinking. If you think differently, you might be viewed as someone who is negative. As Michael Caine said in *The Italian Job*, 'It's a very difficult job and the only way to get through it is we all work together as a team. And that means you do everything I say.' Positive thinking doesn't take away the tough times we have to get through and neither does it make other things happen. There's more to it than that. I have to make choices, plan and do something towards what I want to achieve. I've got to remain flexible and adapt, which I know is no easy task. Facing issues and problems with honesty and realism is, to me, taking a positive approach. Never mind positive thinking; take positive action! If we think and do nothing, chances are nothing will change. It's more about perspective and heading towards our strengths that changes the situation.

Perspective is, in my view, a quality to be treasured and nurtured. I could look at others and myself and see a disability. I could observe the worst. I could scratch just the surface. But autism isn't an illness or disease and it doesn't lead people to commit the terrible criminal acts the newspapers link to people with autism. You see, perspective allows me to take a different approach. I can stop seeing the disability and start to appreciate the gift. I can observe the best and not the worst. I can see the significant and not just what's on the surface.

How does this fit in with the title of this chapter, 'The World Needs Autism'? Well, let's start by asking ourselves the question, 'What's the advantage of having autism?' A different perspective, I know. But let's explore the question.

Let's entertain the notion that there is, somewhere, an advantage to be enjoyed.

You see, I think that some things that start off as a disadvantage in childhood can be nurtured to become something useful. Remember what Thomas Edison said? 'Just because something doesn't do what you planned it to do doesn't mean it's useless.' Nurturing means I'm not going to stamp out every occurrence of a behaviour just because I think it doesn't fit. I think autism is God's gift to mankind's gene pool – it's just mankind hasn't embraced the idea or adopted a balanced perspective that sees beyond 'disabilities' or differences. Step back for a moment and consider the following things.

Repetition and precision can produce consistency and focus to obtain a result

I used to say that women believe most men have ADD – attention deficit disorder – because they don't give them much attention. Most men think women have OCD – obsessive complaining disorder! But that wouldn't be surprising if the men neglected to give their wives or girlfriends the attention they need. When it comes to repetition and obsessive behaviours, it's easy to just see them as annoying or pernickety. Yet some jobs such as computer programming, engineering, research and accounting would consider the ability to repeat things over and over again a real advantage. In fact, precision and exactness are essential in research. I have a joke at work at Christmas. I admit it's cruel but I can't resist. Every year the accountants at my firm decorate a Christmas tree in reception. Everything is precise – blue and silver decorations symmetrically arranged on the tree. It has to be just so. What I do, when no one is looking, is replace a bauble with a multicoloured one and change some of the symmetry. It annoys the hell out of them and they've not worked out it's me (yet!). Every Christmas the phantom strikes again. At home I insist on letting our children decorate the tree any way they wish (which annoys my wife).

A special interest or obsession can be substituted for motivation and passion in a field of expertise

Ever wondered how someone got to be so good at something or how they got their expertise and knowledge? Obsession! Passion! Excessive motivation! The very things we thought would hold a child back are the very things we need in the world today. Take a look around you – I bet the inventions you see are the result of someone's obsession or special interest.

Someone once said to the 26th US President, Theodore Roosevelt, 'Mr Roosevelt, you are a great man!' With characteristic honesty, he replied, 'No, Teddy Roosevelt is simply a plain, ordinary man – highly motivated.' Get it? From an ordinary person who has motivation or passion something can be achieved.

There's another interesting point to note. Sometimes people with expertise can be relied upon when we listen to their opinion. If they say something will work, you know it will. That's such a valuable asset – someone who can be clear and definitive in their convictions because of their expertise. They just have to be given the opportunity to say what they think without fear or interruption from dominant people who don't think things through so thoroughly.

Perfectionism can reveal an ability for attention to detail

Sometimes it's the little things that make the difference. An eye for detail means we can spot what someone's missed or failed to grasp. I love the *Colombo* detective series because this scruffy, unkempt and non-standard police officer likes to see things for himself and always works out who the criminal is because he spots what others miss. The small details matter.

Not fitting in can lead on to an ability to work alone

I've always felt at home not fitting in. I've learned to work in a team but I shine when a task is mine to own. Many employers and schools encourage teamwork as if it's the most important thing. But let's be balanced. We need team players and we also need individuals who will just get on with the task. No idle talk and passing the blame – they produce the results.

Doing things differently can blossom into creativity and inventiveness

You've got to let them explore. One of my children's maths teachers once commented that they observed that my child 'played with numbers'. They knew the answer to a problem but wanted to explore. The teacher got it right when she said, 'I tolerate it because I'm interested in what they're doing.' One of my daughters approached art in a different way too. She'd photograph an object, manipulate the digital image's colours on a computer and print it out. She'd then produce a pastel picture on paper. A different way of processing led to a new creativity. Do you see the positive? Millions saw the apple fall but it was Isaac Newton who asked, 'Why?'

Lacking emotion may enable the completion of a task that needs detachment

Think of jobs where emotional detachment can be an advantage. It doesn't mean the person doesn't care, but detachment helps them to be more efficient. Doctors, lawyers, undertakers, policemen, judges and ambulance crew all need at times to remain emotionally detached so they can get a job done to the best of their ability.

Imagine you have a crisis. Out of two people who could help you, one is very emotional and the other seems more detached. Both have the same skills and abilities, but the solution requires focus and full concentration. Who would you choose?

Being socially inappropriate can make situations interesting, fun and a little less boring – even a little crazy!

Someone once asked my wife, 'What's it like living with him?' Her reply about life with me was 'Sometimes it's a little crazy'.

It's probably true from her perspective. I'm predictable, but there are occasions when my reactions to things are unexpected. Sometimes I'm funny and other times I'm annoying or maddening. But mostly funny! (In my opinion.)

Who wants an ordinary life? Most people I talk to seem to want something different in a relationship, and you sure get that if your spouse or partner has an autistic spectrum condition. There are many comedians on the spectrum as well as more serious business people. Many are probably not diagnosed, but I'd like to think a diagnosis would help in a relationship and free the individual to understand themselves better and to live in the positive aspects of their gift.

I have to admit to being quite serious as a child, although I had a sense of humour which stayed locked away. I was quite intense and focussed on my studies, but as I entered my 30s I began to relax more and have fun. I've learned to enjoy spontaneity and unexpected surprises. I've let the humour out and I worry less what people say about it. You know what? It makes life fun for me and for others too.

Concluding, then, I could write about famous people who are on the autistic spectrum who have achieved a great deal. Undoubtedly, autism has enabled the invention of phones, computers and technology, and has helped to find breakthroughs in science or engineering. But such examples might not help you in your situation. If you're a parent or carer, your child probably isn't an Albert Einstein or Isaac Newton. But could you dare to believe he or she may have something you need to nurture that could make a difference in their life and in the lives of others?

Are you beginning to see past the disability and starting to appreciate the gift?

13

All it Takes is a Little Bit of … Faith

'Faith is taking the first step even when you don't see the whole staircase.'

MARTIN LUTHER KING

There's a story about a man who is visiting a village and decides to stop at the local pub for a cold drink. As he approaches the pub, a nun stops him, points her finger at him and says, 'Don't go in there! Think of your mother and father! Think of the evils of drink!'

The man steps back and thinks for a moment and then asks, 'How do you know drink is evil? Have you ever tried it?'

The nun replies angrily, 'Of course not!'

'Listen,' the man replies. 'I don't mind you complaining about things you've tried, but if you've never had a drink, you can't be telling everyone it's evil. Let me buy you a drink, and if you try it and still think it's evil, I'll accept what you say.'

'Well, all right then,' the nun replies.

'What would you like?' the man asks.

'I don't know. What do women usually have?' the nun enquires.

'A gin and tonic is quite popular. I'll buy you one of those,' he replies.

The man is just about to go in when the nun says, 'Wait a minute! Make sure you get them to put it in a tea cup. I don't want people to think I'm drinking gin and tonic.'

The man agrees and goes inside. He approaches the barman and asks, 'Could I have a pint of your best bitter and a gin and tonic, please?'

'Certainly, sir,' the barman answers.

'Oh, and could you put the gin and tonic in a tea cup, please?' the man almost forgets to ask.

The barman turns and exclaims, 'Good heavens! Don't tell me that crazy nun has come back again!'

I'm not going to tell you that God loves you. I'm not going to tell you that Jesus died on a cross so you can experience forgiveness and peace, and I'm not going to tell you that God makes the difference in everyday life. These are things I think you'd want to find out for yourself. You don't need another preacher telling you what you should or should not believe. Why? Because freedom means we are allowed to choose.

But would you mind if I share with you some things that have helped me? They are deeply personal so it's not easy to take what is precious and open myself up to criticism, anger or ridicule. Yes, these are the reactions that are quite common when some people share their little bit of faith. I hope you don't mind. I promise not to preach at you – only encourage. I'm choosing to take the risk despite some people's reaction because I think you're worth it. You've come this far and I'm asking, if you want to, to come a little further to the end of the book. The choice is up to you. You can either end the book here or find out how a little bit of faith has helped me. I won't be offended if you stop at this point because I know these things are challenging. I really hope I've encouraged you and the next paragraph will mark the start of the last part of the book. You can always come back to it later because you have the freedom of choice. Read it in secret if you like. Whatever you choose, I want to thank you for taking time to read what I've written and I hope I've managed to help you. I really do wish you well.

I want to thank you for staying with me. I'm honoured and privileged that you want to hear my story. You see, faith for me isn't about pie in the sky when you die but steak on a plate while you wait. Faith is for now. Faith has to work. It has to be real.

When I was 13 years old, I firmly asserted myself as an atheist. Science had the answers. While other kids were playing football and not giving the whole debate any consideration, there was I debating with my own mind. The problem was I had a deep sense of needing to be forgiven. I'm not sure why I felt that way, because my family didn't attend any church. My grandmother was the only one I knew who went to church and she believed it should be fun. Today I love that idea! Although I didn't believe in God, I wanted a career as a vicar. That had to be the weirdest combination. How can you become a representative of God when you don't believe God exists? When I look back, I sometimes wonder if God was playing with me and having a bit of fun.

At 14 I had to choose my examination subjects and religious education was suggested. I accepted the idea, knowing I was pretty awful at geography and history. To pass the subject I had to complete a project on any topic from any religion. Since my cousin was being christened, I opted to write about the history of baptism. An ironic choice when I was trying to escape history.

The project meant a trip to Stratford-upon-Avon to watch the christening and a trip to a friend's Baptist church where someone was being baptised as an adult in a pool. I found my cousin's christening interesting and the church building was impressive, but I wasn't any more convinced about God's existence. There was no parting of the water in the font or burst of an angelic choir on the scene. In fact, the family gathering of about ten people didn't produce a heavenly sound at all.

The Baptist church was going to be different, I was told. So I was nervous and thought maybe I wouldn't go. My friend was persistent and said the experience would help my project. Reluctantly, I agreed and one Sunday evening I sat quietly with my friend and a group of other young people. They all seemed to want to be there and the place was packed. Somewhat different from the ten people at my cousin's christening!

I can't remember very much about the service except that the person being baptised didn't drown. She was placed completely under the water! I also remember the singing was very loud as everyone joined in with enthusiasm. The speaker went on about something, but all I can remember is that he said his life was like a rose bush. But instead of producing roses, he kept on growing thorns. He was implying that everything seemed to go wrong, which struck a chord with me. He was describing my life! As long as I could remember, I always seemed to end up in trouble or things just didn't go right. I was the unluckiest kid in town.

I had plenty of material for my school project but I was left wondering why these people wanted to go to church. There was no forcing of religion down my throat and no one told me what to believe. Instead, people were kind and welcoming, which was something I wasn't accustomed to. One man shook my hand and thanked me for coming to the service. He gave me a booklet to read and I left with my friend. For some reason I was offended that someone gave me a booklet about faith; although I'd said I was an atheist,

I still considered myself a Christian because I lived as good a life as possible. My friend explained that no offence would have been meant and that the man was just being kind. I wasn't very good at understanding motives.

That evening, before I went to sleep, I read the booklet. It explained that no one is perfect and that the reason Jesus died on a cross was so that we could be forgiven. God loved the world and wanted people to know Him. Being a Christian isn't primarily about trying to be good. It's about an encounter and meeting with a God who cares. It's about knowing Him. In order to benefit, I needed to change my thinking and accept God was real. That night I prayed and gave up the fight. I accepted God existed and my life changed direction. I found the forgiveness I was looking for.

I woke up the next day knowing my life had changed from the inside. I was excited and I began to tell people. Thing was, others weren't very pleased to hear my news. In fact, they were positively unkind. Not only was I unable to fit in but now that I'd found a little bit of faith I was even more rejected. It was hard, but I saw no logical reason to give up. After all, children with autism tend to see the world in black-and-white terms. If God was real, then that was that.

You might ask if faith is really worth the price. I think so. The advantage faith brings to me far outweighs the cost. I've said that faith needs to be real. It has to work. What I found is that faith does work. It gives me a sense of value and worth. My life matters. What's more interesting is that God doesn't have body language or social cues I have to work out. I'm on a level playing field with everyone else. I don't have to feel inferior.

I mentioned in Chapter 9 that I have faced some very difficult times. Those times came despite finding faith. Faith doesn't exempt us from trouble or difficulties. What I have found is that difficulties have enabled me to grow in character and help others. I've also found that faith helps in the difficulties. I remember going through a very lonely period in my life around the age of 15. Every day was painful and on one afternoon I was standing between my next-door neighbour's hedge and the garage wall. I prayed and asked God for a friend. 'Please make someone call me on the telephone.' Some time passed and I thought I should get on my bicycle and go for a ride. I cycled three miles to the church I attended, but no one was there. Then I thought I should cycle to the park nearby. When I arrived, I saw all the church youth group playing cricket. I had found some company. The strangest thing was that someone came up to me and explained that they were going to telephone me that afternoon but for some reason didn't. Sometimes I think God finds other ways to answer our prayers.

On another occasion I was praying and thought I should go to see the head teacher of my year. I didn't know why and I was too nervous. All I knew was that I had been praying and asking for help to tell all the other students before they left school that God loves them. Later on that week the head teacher summoned me to his office. He told me that he'd been thinking about me and wanted me to read a passage at the leavers' assembly. I bravely asked him if it would be all right to say a few words too and he agreed.

At the leavers' assembly I got to read a passage written by St Paul about rejoicing. I told everyone that although

St Paul knew about hardship, he also knew joy because he was confident that God loved him and cared. Perhaps only a person with autism could have been so upfront and uninhibited because I wouldn't be able to read the other students' body language and be intimidated.

I've advanced the idea that I approach my own autistic mind as a gift because it enables me to do so much. I've encouraged you to take a positive approach too. You might be wondering, 'If there is a God, what's His view?' I've wondered too. Although I don't have the definitive answer to God's point of view, there are examples of characters in the Bible that have impairments. Moses had difficulty speaking, St Paul had some physical affliction, and some people believe even Joseph showed autistic traits. But what about me? Does faith make room for my autism?

In 2014 I gave a lift to a friend to a church meeting in Sussex. It was a gathering of local church leaders and I was the odd one out because I was the chauffeur. Despite this, I was welcome to stay and listen to a guest speaker from Nottingham. It was quite interesting because the lady explained how she had been coping through cancer and what had helped her. In the afternoon she explained that she had brought a friend who had a particular gift to give words of encouragement. Well, her friend went around the room encouraging people and I thought she'd probably miss me out as I was my friend's driver. Thing is, she didn't. I was the last and she sat down at my feet and said the following words: 'Your mind is wired differently. You can read complex things and you get it, you just get it. You're a resource for others.' I'd never met her before and no one in the room knew about my autism to tell her about it. If you read articles about scanning brains with autism, there is evidence the 'wiring' is different. What this tells me is that as far as faith goes, I have a place to serve and help others. I acknowledge I can only speak about my experience but I think it illustrates that faith can help.

In 1997 my unborn daughter was sick. She had a pleural effusion of the left lung which meant fluid was built up in the left lung cavity, preventing her lung from developing and compromising her heart by pushing it well over to the right-hand side. We were referred to St George's Hospital in Tooting where doctors told us they knew of no other children who had survived the condition. Most parents opted for a termination. My wife and I prayed and offered up our daughter as best we could into God's care.

On the Sunday before we went back to the hospital, a lady at church shared a picture she had had in her mind about a hypodermic needle removing the fluid but with no hand on the syringe. The church believed this was God's way of saying He would remove the fluid and our daughter would be delivered safely. When we went back to the hospital, the scans showed the fluid had almost completely drained away. Her heart and lung were back in their place. The doctor admitted he was expecting to have to carry out a procedure to remove the fluid with a needle but was bowled over by the scan. A week later and the scans revealed no trace of the issue and our daughter was born safely that November.

I've always believed people need to make up their own mind about faith. It's not something I would want to force upon them. My children have had the opportunity to learn about what I believe, but my son became addicted to drugs instead. He started smoking tobacco, moved on to cannabis and then on to harder drugs. He had to leave our home so I could keep the family safe, and for several years he lived in temporary accommodation. It was truly heart-breaking. Having autism didn't help him one bit because he was easily influenced by others to take drugs and this became a habit. Yet, despite removing him from our home, I never abandoned him while he was under the care of social services. He was only 17.

I would receive phone calls that he'd been arrested or had moved house, or he had run out of money or was being threatened. It was awful. Then one day, some two years later, I visited him after he had been given a flat. The place was a mess and I cried in front of him. 'It's not meant to be like this,' I told him. The next week I met him for lunch at a Wimpy restaurant where we had the following conversation.

SON: It will be okay.

ME: What will?

SON: Everything.

ME: But it's not okay.

SON: It will be okay because He's watching me.

ME: Who's watching you?

SON: Him up there.

ME: You mean God?

SON: Yes.

ME: You don't believe in God!

SON: Yes I do.

ME: You don't.

SON: I do. He's watching over me.

What I didn't know was that my son had found his own faith and had started to attend a local church. He had to work through his drug issues but today he is free of drugs. It's been a long walk to freedom for him, but his little bit of faith has seen him through. He knows he's vulnerable and I helped him with strategies when he slipped up. Usually, it had to do with being with the wrong crowd or staying around a friend's house too late. Three of his friends died from drugs overdoses, so I'm lucky to have him. When he calls, he tells me he loves me and his mum, and that is such a change. He never verbally expressed love when he was a child.

Whatever people think about faith, faith has helped free my son and that's better than drugs. A change in his beliefs has altered the direction of his life. He and I both have autism and we both have a little bit of faith. Both things help us and those around us. I help and comfort families with children with autism, and my son helps the homeless and those at rock bottom. He's not inhibited or afraid, and I even heard he took a young man trying to give up drugs to his church. He told me the man had Tourette's syndrome and it was a very interesting experience for everyone during the sermon! Faith isn't just about going to a church and singing nice songs or hearing a middle-class sermon. Faith means I roll up my sleeves and wade in to help the most vulnerable when I can.

One last piece of encouragement. Although I have a mind that is autistic, my spirit is free. Autism brings its benefits and strengths, and faith helps me to be free inside from guilt or blame. Some may say I'm idealistic and that's a fair comment. But I'd rather live my life with hope.

Faith reminds me my life matters.

Faith reminds me I'm not alone.

Faith reminds me I can change a life.

I trust the time we've spent together has brought you hope and comfort. We've been realistic about the challenges we face, haven't we? As parents, teachers or people with autism, life throws all sorts of things at us. Our experiences qualify us to help each other through the tough times and we can share the comfort we receive with one another. That's what I've tried to do in this book – share my life and what I've learned so far and add a dose of good humour to lift your spirit. There's only one question left to answer.

'Do lemons have feathers?'

Sometimes all it takes is a little bit of faith.

Help Sheets

Spotting the Possible Signs of Asperger's/ High-Functioning Autism

A	**Attention**	**Attention to detail.** You've noticed they seem to be fixated on one activity or bogged down in the detail. When you have a conversation, they correct minor points or try to be exact. You've noticed they are really knowledgeable on a particular topic but seem disinterested in others. Their speech may be quite advanced and precise for their age.
U	**Understanding**	**Understanding simple instructions is difficult.** You've noticed they just don't get it. They keep asking questions or appear to lack confidence. It seems to take them longer to start a task than everyone else, and finishing a task can be just as difficult. The subtleties of speech and language seem to go over their head so they easily misunderstand instructions.
T	**Trouble**	**Trouble is not far away.** You've noticed that they seem to end up in trouble more than anyone else, even though it seems out of character. They are too honest about what has happened, seem detached from the consequences and cannot explain how things went wrong. They know the rules but don't seem to be able to apply them in different situations.
I	**Isolated**	**Isolated with few friends.** They prefer the company of adults rather than that of their peers. Rarely do they invite friends home and rarely do they go out to see others. At home they spend more time in their bedroom than in the lounge. After being with others, it's not long before they want to withdraw to spend some time alone.
S	**Sensitive**	**Sensitive to the environment around them.** You've noticed they prefer routine and that departing from it causes distress or anger. Their emotions go up and down very easily and something insignificant can cause an emotional meltdown. They are sensitive to touch and even different fabrics. You might even have noticed that they have removed labels from clothes.
M	**Missing**	**Missing social cues.** You've noticed that something is missing. They're intelligent, bright and kind, but they're different. They prefer not to give too much eye contact, and although they are caring, they seem to lack empathy. You might have noticed they are clumsy or lack some motor coordination. You don't want to believe it, but your instinct says something is different.

Strategies to Help People with Asperger's/
High-Functioning Autism

A	Allow	**Allow me extra time to process information, questions and instructions.** My mind is naturally active and looks for the details so that I can carry out an instruction. I might over-analyse things and appear not to be working, or you might think I'm lazy. If I'm not doing what you ask, see if I've understood and explain things again. I'm not stupid – I'm looking for clarity. **Please help me.**
U	Understand	**Understand that I cannot be the same as everyone else.** My brain is wired differently and I cannot do anything to change that. It means that what others find easy (e.g. friendship, communication and social things) I have to be shown and taught. Understand that I have an amazing gift and strengths yet to be discovered. Not all behaviour is bad – sometimes it's just behaviour. **Please help me.**
T	Take	**Take less offence at what I say or do.** I can be very literal in my understanding and can appear blunt or rude. I don't mean to be and I can't always recognise when this happens. I like to ask lots of questions because I'm genuinely interested. A gentle approach to show me how to phrase things and when to ask questions will make all the difference. **Please help me.**
I	Influence	**Influence me for good.** I'm not very good at resisting the 'bad' influence of others but I can be influenced towards good outcomes. Strength of character takes me longer to master and I need to learn about assertiveness. I shy away from conflict and it's easier to go with the crowd. I need positive influences in my life to help me steer a steady course. **Please help me.**
S	Say	**Say what you mean.** I have a tendency to take what you say literally or out of context. It can result in some funny situations but could also annoy you. I'd find it really helpful if you say what you mean so that I don't misinterpret something. Please don't shout at me. So often I get it wrong because I don't pick up social cues or facial expressions, but I'm reassured when you smile. **Please help me.**
M	Mistakes	**Mistakes happen.** I get it wrong even though I try not to. I genuinely want to please people and help out, but knowing how to apply the rules in every situation is hard for me. Sometimes I forget things and just don't know what to do. It makes me worry and feel sad. If you can show how and why something has gone wrong, I can learn. Check if others are enticing me to break the rules. **Please help me.**

Can You Help?

If you've found this book helpful, perhaps you'd like to tell your friends, colleagues and family about it – I'd love to encourage them too.

You might consider rating the book on Amazon.co.uk or putting a post on social media such as Facebook or Twitter. Your support will mean more people will be able to answer the question, 'Do lemons have feathers?'

About the Author

David lives in Sussex with his wife and family. He is a keen supporter of families, schools and children with autism or special needs and works hard to bring people together to find solutions to situations. He is often invited to speak at conferences and parent groups where his positive and humorous insight is both encouraging and fun.

David has also written the very funny book *The Sweet Shop Diaries* under the pseudonym of Walter Jones.

You can contact David by email at:
mastersafe@hotmail.co.uk.